D1215120

THRIVE

THE LEADER'S GUIDE TO BUILDING
A HIGH PERFORMANCE CULTURE

Andrew Freedman
with Paul Elliott, Ph.D

THRIVE

THE LEADER'S GUIDE TO BUILDING A HIGH PERFORMANCE CULTURE

COPYRIGHT © 2021 BY SHIFT MEDIA

All rights reserved. No portion of this book may be reproduced, stored in a retrieval system, or transmitted in any form or by any means—electronic, mechanical, photocopy, recording, scanning, or other—except for brief quotations in critical reviews or articles, without the prior written permission of the publisher.

ISBN

978-1-5445-1607-3 Paperback

9978-1-5445-1608-0 Hard Cover

978-1-5445-1609-7 eBook

DESIGN BY:

Foothold Creative
www.footholdcreative.co

LIONCREST

PUBLISHING

My dearest JoAnn,

You are the life force that
powers me every day.

TABLE OF CONTENTS

THE GENESIS OF THRIVE

Because this book is about change and transformation, and the introspection, resilience, and commitment required to successfully make it, I'm starting it by sharing some things about my personal journey that not many people know—things that set me on a path to thrive in my own life.

I can still remember her reading one of her journal entries to me: "... and every time, I lost another piece of me." She told me that, over time, she had lost so much of herself, that if she did not move forward with this decision, at some point, she'd be gone. Completely gone.

I couldn't breathe.

By my recollection, we had a solid family unit. Although we were not financially rich, my sister and I never wanted for anything. I remember laughter, love, and support while growing up. That my mother was leaving my father floored me. It just did not compute.

My mother read more journal passages to me and shared what her life had really been like over the preceding thirty years. A schoolteacher for more than thirty-six years, she was an exemplar in her profession. Her classes were videotaped to use as training tools for new teachers. She represented teachers in negotiations in her school systems. Students consistently visited her, years after they passed her classes, to tell her what a positive impact she had on their lives. At home, though, things were very different.

We lost our home, saw our father go to jail, had creditors calling us every day for as long as I can remember, and for over fifteen years, my mom worked two jobs just to be sure we could make ends meet. I was aware of these things but did not realize the cumulative toll it had all taken on my mom. She had been eroding, bit by bit, incident by incident. She had even weathered finding out that my father had cheated on her. In fact, I came to understand that he got married to another woman while married to my mom. Drop the mic.

At first, I was enraged at what I learned as she bared her soul to me. That rage then turned to even deeper levels of respect and admiration for her. She had made the choice to stay married for over thirty years, regardless of the circumstances, to ensure her kids had a solid foundation, and the love, support, and education they needed to achieve success in their lives. Until she didn't. Until she hit a breaking point, one based in a refusal to completely shed who she was—as a mother, as a woman, as a human. At that breaking point, she reclaimed her life and left my father. My mom has been one of my most important role models for doing what is right, living life with an open mind and heart, trusting freely, and generously giving time, energy, and effort, regardless of what would come in return. As she shared all of this with me, I could see the trajectory of my life change ahead of me.

In that moment, everything became so clear, so easy. I reflected on my life, who I was, what I stood for, and my current situation. I resolved myself to never settle for anything that did not absolutely set my soul on fire. This meant jobs, friendships, hobbies, vacations, and most definitely personal relationships. Very soon after this time with my mom, I filed for a divorce.

I was in a bad marriage that was only getting worse. I had been making bad personal and financial choices, choosing destructive self-soothing methods, and telling myself that I deserved what was going wrong in my life. The reality was that if I had not stopped tolerating my own poor mindset and behavior, I would have gone down a very dark path, likely worse than what my mother had traveled. I made a commitment to myself that I would not accept a reality wherein I didn't behave like the person I knew I really was: good, honest, true, trusting, and here to bring out the greatness in others.

No more playing small, playing scared, and playing the victim. I knew the way forward meant fully immersing myself in the things that absolutely lit me up. A life where every day, I would wake up inspired to help others have an existence that left them feeling more alive, not less; more connected to others, not more distant from them; more passionate about their careers, not more disengaged; and more fulfilled in life, not emptier.

Soon after this realization and commitment, I knew that for me to bring this vision to reality, I had to operate at scale. Impacting one person at a time did light me up, but it was not enough. I was destined for more. I changed my career path so I could be a catalyst for more growth and impact. That is what brought me to SHIFT. I understood that the art and science of building high-performing company cultures is intrinsically related to helping people find their purpose.

Through this work, I see leaders change their mindsets about what is possible for their organizations. I see them reach higher levels of performance on a consistent basis. I see businesses transform before my eyes, becoming magnets for top talent, surpassing goals that they once thought were impossible.

This was when Paul and I started collaborating on strategic initiatives with clients to help them apply the high-performance principles and practices that facilitated growth and business impact. We were onto something powerful, and yet we were just getting started. The story was just beginning to be written. Now Paul and I have decided to share with the world what we know to be true about transforming performance and business results. Our purpose is clear: to help the world THRIVE.

Here we are. Together. Let's do this.

INTRODUCTION

If you are working on something exciting
that you really care about, you don't have
to be pushed. The vision pulls you.

—STEVE JOBS

Imagine a world where your employees can't wait to get to work every day. They are inspired, fired up by the mission and vision of the company, challenged and energized by their role, and supported by an aligned leadership team. Where, on the thousandth day of work, each individual's drive to excel surpasses that of their first day on the job, and that drive is made obvious by their results—they consistently exceed expectations.

This world doesn't need to exist only in your imagination; we know it can be your reality.

Unfortunately, the opposite often occurs. Employees experience their work environments as negative and stifling. They often coast through the tasks, unable to know if their work even mattered or if they had a winning day. Business results reflect this: revenue targets are missed, initiatives and projects fail to deliver the intended ROI, profits remain stagnant or decline, and everyone is working harder for diminishing returns.[1]

Ample research over the past eighteen years, including studies done by organizations including Deloitte, Accenture, and our firm, SHIFT, shows that 70 percent of the American workforce is disengaged at work. Whether or not you are familiar with the research, you know what disengagement looks like.

Almost 55 percent of the disengaged population show up as *sleepwalkers*. Sleepwalkers are not connected to the firm's mission. They are unclear about and disinterested in the relationship between their role and creating value for customers. They arrive late to work on a regular basis. Instead of taking ownership for project tasks or performance goals, they point to external factors as the basis for failing to meet expectations. Sleepwalkers have a "check the box" mentality as they seek to just get through the day.

As unproductive as sleepwalkers are, 15 percent of the disengaged population live as something much more dangerous—*saboteurs*. Saboteurs actively work against company goals. They try to get back at their boss, colleagues, clients, or company. Their worldview includes

1. "United States Nonfarm Labour Productivity," Trading Economics, https://tradingeconomics.com/united-states/productivity.

the perspective that someone did them wrong (e.g., they were unfairly passed over for a promotion or not given opportunities that others have in life). As opposed to looking inward to see how they can improve themselves or the situation, saboteurs try to throw a monkey wrench into the system. They hold informal "meetings after the meeting" to unwind or undermine company decisions, and they refuse to comply with company policies. They may take an "it's not my job," stance when it comes to solving customer-related issues. Look around. You've got them. Saboteurs exist in every organization at every level.

Connected to the unacceptable volume of disengaged employees, research also shows that 70 percent of business transformation and change initiatives fail to deliver the intended results.[2] This includes failed mergers, system integrations, new product rollouts, and workforce productivity initiatives. Time after time, companies miss deadlines, have budget overruns, and don't deliver the promised business value. The barriers to higher levels of engagement and performance seem to be everywhere.

There is hope. At SHIFT, our mission is to shift the American workforce from 70 percent disengaged to 70 percent engaged. When people are engaged at work, they go home happier, healthier, and fulfilled. Employee engagement is a positive, purposeful, passionate state of mind. It allows people to build something greater than themselves. We believe business is the spark that will ignite this change.

We can do better. Let us show the way. *THRIVE* is your blueprint.

CREATING A CULTURE OF HIGH ENGAGEMENT AND HIGH PERFORMANCE

Start with the premise that people are naturally curious and creative, and want to do good work. They want to engage, achieve, make prog-

2. "Why Change Initiatives Fail," Kenan-Flagler Business School, https://www.imd.org/research-knowledge/articles/10-reasons-why-organizational-change-fails/

ress, consistently perform at high levels, and feel proud. They want to *thrive*. When leaders create cultures, systems, and processes that foster these opportunities, employees more fully engage and are more likely to achieve maximum performance at work.

Envision your people as having an insatiable passion and drive for creating a "triple-win" relationship for the organization, employees, and customers. The customer experience is optimized, and the organization reaches its goals. These employees thrive—committed to the organization, energized by their work, and having created countless opportunities for themselves and others to succeed.

At SHIFT, we believe that consistent high performance stems from having a barrier-free work environment. In this kind of environment, people can perform at their best because of the work systems, as opposed to having to work around or despite those work systems. There is absolute clarity about the purpose and value of each employee's role, and how that role impacts the organization. Through *THRIVE*, we will provide you with the framework to make this a reality in your organization. We emphasize the intersection of engagement and performance in this introduction, because it is vital to the success of a company—it is the key to creating a thriving organization.

Before we move on, it is important for us to do a gut check. If you are thinking, "I already have a totally engaged workforce" or "My organization is already high performing; we are doing just fine," please put this book down. If you think you already know everything you need to know about building a winning organization, please put this book down. This book is for those who know that every organization has upside potential, even if it is already stable and profitable. Even industry leaders can keep getting better. In fact, their commitment to continuous evolution is an underlying component of the success they refuse to be seduced by. Companies that claim to have a high-performing culture likely do have pockets of high performance, but it's not embedded across the entire enterprise.

To transform your organization, company leaders need to be clear about and consistently express what matters most, and what the measures of success look like. They need to answer questions like "What does impact look like? What is the purpose of the company? What is the company trying to accomplish?" (Hint: it is more than just profit.) True engagement begins with a focus on the critical elements and influences of high performance, and a clear definition of success is one of those elements.

A high-performing organization must create a system that attracts the right people and repels the wrong ones. These high-performance systems are clear and consistent about your beliefs through your mission, vision, and values. High-performing organizations rely on leaders who openly demonstrate the thinking and behavior that align with these articulations of excellence and success. You can't build high-performing teams without high-performing leaders. It all starts with leadership.

GETTING THE MOST OUT OF THIS BOOK

This book is not about finding perpetual joy in the workplace—it's about truth. Truth through looking in the mirror to understand what accelerates and also decelerates engagement and performance. As Richard Saul Wurman, founder of TED, said, "Understanding precedes action." Before you launch one more engagement campaign, change one more compensation plan, install one more new policy or procedure that you think will fix perceived issues, you must first understand the truth. The truth is that the issue may not be your employees. It may start with *you*.

This book is for leaders who want to understand what really drives high performance and how to replicate that performance throughout the entire organization. We wrote *THRIVE* for continuous learners who are tired of failed initiatives and are no longer satisfied with the status quo or even comparison to existing benchmark data. This book is for CEOs, COOs, CSOs, CHROs, CXOs, and other high-level executives who are tasked with formulating and/or implementing organizational strategies and know that it is time to think and execute differently—they want to *be* the benchmark. If you don't play one of those roles (yet) but want to learn what it takes to build a high-performance culture, read on. This will be an invaluable blueprint for you.

If you move forward on the path we outline, you must fully commit to this process of change. For example, it is easy to distribute an employee engagement survey or create a new role definition—companies do these things all the time. Distributing a survey is only one act; it is like putting one foot forward, but not really having gone anywhere yet. It's not holistic enough to bring about sustained change and impact. Employees complete the survey, leaders aren't sure what the next steps should be, and so nothing changes.

If you ask for input, *be ready to act*. Asking employees what they think and then not acting based on their feedback makes things worse. If you ask and do nothing, it suggests that you really do not care what they think, and that can absolutely kill employee morale. Don't ask if you don't plan to implement changes. We cannot emphasize this enough: change is hard. Sustained change and transformation, especially in large organizations, takes focused, consistent effort, dedicated resources, and sustained executive sponsorship. Most transformation efforts we undertake span at least three to five years. Do you have the grit and resilience for that journey? We know you do.

This book—this blueprint—should be a catalyst for action. Here is the suggested progression:

- Read *THRIVE* from cover to cover. Don't write notes, and don't highlight any text. Don't take action while reading.

- Read the book a second time. This time, we suggest you make notes as you go, cataloguing your thoughts on where and how you can apply the principles, frameworks, methodologies, tools, and templates. Jump around to the parts that had the most resonance with you during the first read. Explore the THRIVE Accelerators, as they are tools and templates that you can use immediately. Take time to complete the THRIVE Reflections, as they will give you to time to examine what is happening in your organization and how you can make things even better. Then go back, review your notes, and prioritize accordingly.

- Based on your prioritized list, dig back into specific sections and create precise action plans for impact.

THRIVE ACCELERATORS AND REFLECTIONS

Throughout the book, you will see **THRIVE Accelerators** and **THRIVE Reflections**. Each of these plays an important role in your extracting the most value possible from *THRIVE*.

⚡ THRIVE ACCELERATORS:

These are tools, templates, or examples that bring a specific high-performance concept or process to life. When you see the lightning bolt icon, this indicates that an Accelerator exists for your use. You can access each Accelerator by visiting thrive.shiftthework.com/accelerators, so you can apply it in your organization. You'll encounter your first Accelerator, the 25 Reasons Why, in a few pages.

💡 THRIVE REFLECTION:

These are interactive exercises that we encourage you to use while reading *THRIVE*. Applying critical thought to these questions will accelerate your ability to recognize the biggest opportunities for you to shift performance in your organization. When you see the light bulb icon, this indicates that it is time for purposeful reflection.

CASE IN ACTION

An industry-leading firm had experienced significant growth through acquisition over time and, by many standards, outperformed industry peers. They met Wall Street projections, had many long-tenured employees throughout their ranks, and took great pride in their financial performance. However, as they looked at their current and future business health indicators and the changing industry landscape, some of the executives became very concerned. They saw significant attrition in key roles. They were unable to attract new employees, and attempts to recruit top talent were often met with hesitation or rejection by the candidates. Hiring managers learned that candidates heard negative things about the firm through the industry grapevine.

After a series of rejections from potential hires and increased levels of regrettable attrition, it became obvious to this company that their command-and-control approach wasn't serving them well in the moment, and it most certainly wouldn't allow them to thrive in the years ahead. In fact, their leadership methods had earned them a bad reputation. They knew that becoming a magnet for top talent needed to be a critical component of their organizational strategy, so they reached out to our company, SHIFT, for help.

This company was serious and took a big step forward in accepting our help. We began with a company-wide "voice of the employee" survey. We went deep into the organization—to the frontline employees who were closest to the customers in a variety of their markets. We needed to connect with the people who did the day-to-day work. The survey addressed the areas of culture, strategy, people, and talent—all critical elements in creating a high-performance organization. With respect to the people, as an example, we examined multiple phases of the employee life cycle, including:

- Recruiting, hiring, and onboarding practices
- Learning and development
- Levels of connection between employees and managers
- Role clarity and goal alignment
- Performance management

Once the survey was complete, we distilled reams of data into the highest-impact actionable recommendations for the executives. This was so we could align on the most direct path to increase engagement, elevate performance, and attract and retain top talent—we aimed to create a barrier-free work environment.

If we had simply walked in and told the executives what to do, without involving the frontline employees, the best we could have hoped for was compliance to executive directives. Engaging and enrolling people in a process creates buy-in; people will put their blood, sweat, and tears into a movement they helped to author, and they will own and celebrate the success of that endeavor.

We needed to give the employees a voice. We shared our recommendations at a meeting with over one hundred company leaders, and we asked them to prioritize the top ten things that needed to be done to accomplish those goals. After they prioritized, we randomly split the employees into different work groups; each group was responsible for taking ownership of one of the critical areas for improvement. Since these employees voiced the particular issues or challenges, they were perfect to help create the solution.

The groups made significant progress. They came up with new programs to recognize top performers. They created three new retention and growth strategies to help them keep their best people. They designed a new, more effective onboarding process for new employees. They revamped their mission, vision, and values. In less than a year, they built and implemented these new programs and methods across the entire organization.

The company has made significant progress toward their desired goals and continues working every day to improve. Even better, the employees continue finding new ways that they, individually, can help the company thrive. We don't take full credit for what they've accomplished, but using the elements from the blueprint contained in this book, we did help them make significant progress, and they now continue to experience the benefits of these improvements, while working on new ways to get even better.

THE EXEMPLARY PERFORMANCE SYSTEM

Paul designed the Exemplary Performance System (EPS), the framework we use to help leaders view the world through a different lens. It helps create a path to process improvement, employee engagement, and consistent, higher levels of performance. The six influences of the EPS originated from the work of Tom Gilbert, psychologist and author of the book *Human Competence*, and focus on enabling people to produce results. With admiring acknowledgment to Gilbert, we have taken the framework and run with it, making it one of the foundations of our work. We will reference it frequently throughout the book. Each category helps us think systemically about the work of an organization.

The six influences within the EPS can either facilitate or impede performance. They are interdependent, and when aligned, they provide the foundation for a maximum shift in performance. The influences are listed below:

- Environments, Systems, and Resources
- Expectations and Feedback
- Rewards, Recognition, and Consequences
- Capacity and Job Fit
- Skills and Knowledge
- Motivation and Preferences

Looking at the graphic, the three influences across the top are external to the performer. The bottom three influences are internal to an individual and are impacted by external factors that exist within the company. These six categories of influences provide a framework for creating a high-performance culture. How the influences take shape is determined by each organization.

FIGURE I.1

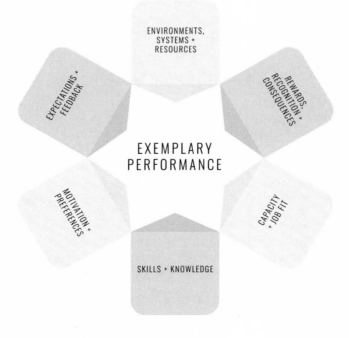

ENVIRONMENTS, SYSTEMS + RESOURCES

EXPECTATIONS + FEEDBACK

REWARDS, RECOGNITION, + CONSEQUENCES

EXEMPLARY PERFORMANCE

MOTIVATION + PREFERENCES

CAPACITY + JOB FIT

SKILLS + KNOWLEDGE

We realize that different people inside an organization may own one or more of the six influences of the EPS. Each owner does the best she can with her part, attempting to positively impact the entire organizational system. Investing all resources into any one category will not create a high-performance culture. As systems theory states, Optimizing a subsystem will suboptimize the system. It's only when all six subsystems are fully integrated that the desired results emerge.

The EPS can be used to create a barrier-free work environment that is accessible to all. In such an environment, work systems and all business processes are designed with the intent of exceptional organizational and individual performance. For example, recruiting posts and job descriptions align perfectly with performance expectations, and onboarding, training, and ongoing development enable targeted performance acceleration that aligns directly to the organization's critical business goals. Rewards and recognition correspond appropriately to employee accomplishments. The right tools and resources are available at the right time and in ways that accelerate performance. Systems and processes are designed with the performer in mind, enabling smoother workflow and better business results. Regardless of where you are today, your path to higher levels of performance will reveal itself as you read this book.

EYES WIDE OPEN

Tremendous sacrifice. Gut-wrenching pain. Cold sweats that wake you up in the middle of the night. Massive resistance and self-doubt that make you question your resilience and fortitude. You can expect to experience all of this and more along the path to creating a thriving organization.

If you truly want to create a thriving, high-performance culture, you must fully commit from the depths of your soul and with every fiber of your being, and you must begin now. As musical artists Salt-N-Pepa once said, "This dance ain't for everybody, only the sexy people." Well, maybe "sexy" isn't a requirement for achieving consistent levels of high performance, but we can say that not all leaders are ready for what it takes to thrive. Use the following three prompts to reflect upon whether you are ready to give what it takes to successfully shift engagement and performance.

FIND YOUR *WHY*:

To create a thriving organization, leaders must have a clear purpose. Why is shifting performance an absolute nonnegotiable? Complete the **25 Reasons Why** exercise to gain more insight into what is most important to you. You must have clarity on this piece before starting this journey.

 Download at thrive.shiftthework.com/accelerators

SET THE "EXPECTED CONDITIONS":

Make a list of all the things that you and your people will likely experience throughout the transformation, including sacrificing time, money, energy, sleep, ego, other initiatives (you can have it all, you just can't do it all), and relationships (it's likely that some people will need to exit from your company if they can't make the needed shifts through this process). At the same time, you'll also experience joy, triumph, learning, progress, and growth. You'll want to refer to these expected conditions throughout your organization's transformation. They will serve to remind you and your team that you knew this wouldn't be easy, and it will be worth it. You need to not only weather the tough conditions during this process but also welcome them with open arms. Not ready? That's okay. Keep reading this book, even if it's not time for you to pull the trigger on a high-performance transformation just yet.

DRAFT A TEAM OF HIGH-PERFORMANCE NINJAS:

This kind of organizational change requires significant help. Who will help you bring your vision to fruition? Make a list of the skills and competencies needed to drive this transformation so you tap the right people to mobilize the effort. Of note, to accelerate effectiveness in a mission of this magnitude, you will need a blend of fully dedicated internal resources, not just fractional ones. Additionally, you will want to leverage outside expertise and resources. This approach helps to eliminate possible biases that existing leaders and employees tend to have—biases that may prevent them from being objective in analysis, evaluation, and execution. A fresh approach and a fresh set of eyes, combined with expertise, adds value and accuracy to the overall process. If you cannot envision your team, you've got more work to do before starting your high-performance crusade.

We have heard leaders express concern about the time and commitment that business transformation efforts take, especially from high-performing employees. There's no getting around it—you need to apply some of your best and brightest thinking to this effort. The greater concern should be whether you can afford to allow excessive performance variance in critical roles to persist. Regardless of how much revenue or profit your company produces, you can always, and we mean always, have more impact. After implementing the EPS, we normally see a 20 to 30 percent reduction in the variance across critical roles. Imagine what that would do to your top and bottom lines. If you run current performance numbers, the calculation will affirm that you can't afford to not shift performance in the ways we know are possible.

If your business is struggling, you feel like you've got too much going on, or don't have the right team to make a successful transformation happen, now is an important time to establish what success looks like for the organization. Consider what it will take to win, and what high performance looks like in the critical roles that power your organization. Our approach can be an accelerator to amplify results, shifting your organization from one that simply survives to one that thrives. At the same time, if your company is experiencing success, this could help you maximize impact. We've had leaders show us their balance sheets and industry awards, stating that they are already high performing and that their revenue and profits are already healthy. Thriving is about not being satisfied with the status quo, and it isn't enough to be an industry leader. Think about previous industry leaders and "good to great" companies that no longer exist. Even if you have a winning formula, think about the impact, revenue, and profit you may still be leaving on the table. Why wouldn't you want to shift performance and maximize impact for your clients, employees, and community?

As you start to dig into the book, you may have a blend of excitement and trepidation, creating uncertainty about whether this is the right time to implement our performance system in your organization. Regardless of your apparent level of readiness, the answer is "Yes, now is absolutely the right time." Regardless. The answer is not "As soon as we solve this next challenge, we'll be ready," or "As soon as we hit this next milestone and make this next team transition, we can do this." That is neither high-performance thinking nor the foundation for a thriving organization. Think back to why you accepted your role. Consider why it is critical for you, your team, and your company to thrive. Think about the employees, and their families, that are counting on you to lead the company forward. We know you can do this, and we know you understand the logic behind why it is critical for you to help your company evolve in the ways we've described. This journey can be akin to a person committed to creating vibrant health walking into a health club, and saying, "This club looks good. I like the programs and the equipment. The club is clean, and the price is right. As soon as I lose twenty pounds, I'll join." That mindset and thinking are flawed—if that individual could have lost twenty pounds, he would have already done so. He also knows that if it really is critical for him to lose the twenty pounds, he must start doing things differently. Leaders need to stop unintentionally getting in their own way. If they could have elevated engagement and performance to even better levels using current processes and models, they would have done so already. Many leaders need help accepting the reality that they do need help to transform their organization to a high-performance culture. Change and transformation are hard, with over 70 percent of transformation initiatives failing to deliver the intended results. The science behind driving high performance is not widely known, and sometimes it just isn't possible for organizations to do this work on their own.

When we were introduced to a financial services company, they told us, "There's never been a more critical time for us to get our organization clear and aligned on our priorities. We need to redefine key roles and corresponding responsibilities, reconstruct our sales territories, and modify our compensation programs, but we just don't have capacity." They knew they needed to transform performance in a sustainable way, but they didn't have the resources to do it on their own. We aligned on what success would look like for them, forged a great partnership, and became an expanded resource for their critical, high-performance mission. While most business transformation efforts fail, you can beat the odds. There is always a way to make the shift real for yourself and your organization.

We intend **THRIVE** *to spur creative thought, moments of inspiration and clarity, and insights into how you can build a higher-performing culture. To facilitate this process, we have strategically placed THRIVE Reflection sections, where we pose questions for your consideration. When you encounter a Reflection section, we suggest you pause, clear your mind, and answer each question honestly and fully. In doing so, you will more clearly see the areas where you can focus to make the most significant shifts in engagement and performance in your organization. Here is your first opportunity.*

Is your organization involved in a major strategic initiative that will dramatically impact the future?

Do you have a model or process in place to increase the probability that the initiative(s) will land successfully and have the desired business impact?

Do you have the internal bandwidth to address change in a holistic way?

Do you see material performance variance within specific roles (across teams or regions) that are critical to your organizational goals and strategies?

In what areas of your business are you coasting?

What is preventing you from doing the greatest work of your life?

HOW THIS BOOK IS ORGANIZED

Section I of this book illustrates the shift required to create a high-performance culture and workplace. It provides philosophy, research data, and real-life experiences. It illuminates what is possible.

- **Chapter 1: Define Success** explains why alignment of business goals and roles is important to creating a thriving organization.

- **Chapter 2: Organizational Influences** introduces you to three key influences and related factors that inhibit or foster success.

- **Chapter 3: Individual Performance** discusses specific performance influences, how they are impacted by organizational influences, and what facilitates exceptional performance.

- **Chapter 4: Analyze "Star" Employees** presents little known truths about star employees and introduces you to the Role Excellence Profile (REP) process, which can provide greater role clarity for individual contributors and teams, identify best practices, and uncover barriers to high performance.

Section I is intended to get you *unstuck*—to kick you out of your current (comfortable) mindset. Use this section as a prompt to conduct an internal analysis of your organization. This section is a diagnostic tool.

Section II is a step-by-step guide—showing you how to create a thriving organization. Here, you'll get what you need to make significant shifts in performance.

- **Chapter 5: Amplify and Accelerate Impact and Results** discusses how to effectively cascade strategies and goals throughout your organization, while shifting the odds in favor of successful business transformation and change.

- **Chapter 6: Implement Strategy** shows you how to create a system of planning and system of engagement. It will help you establish the rituals, routines, and rhythms necessary to implement strategic changes and to more fully engage employees at all levels.

- **Chapter 7: Resistance and Resilience** explains how resistance shows up in an organization and how to build resilience during times of change and transformation.

Use Section II to develop your plan to consistently elevate company and employee performance. However, this section won't be of much benefit to you if you have yet to change your mindset around what it takes to build a high-performance culture.

Make the shift and get ready to see your organization thrive!

WHERE ARE YOU TODAY?

The truth does not change according
to our ability to stomach it.

—FLANNERY O'CONNOR

 SECTION 1 ACCELERATORS

THE MAP

QUALITY REFERENCE CHECKS

24 COMMON BIASES

This high-performance journey on which you are about embark requires you to get your head in the right space (we call this "getting your head on right"). To help you do this, take a few minutes and answer the following questions (this is a ritual we call The Map; more on rituals later in the book):

- How *are* you? (In considering this, think about your mental and physical health, your mindset, your focus, and your energy.)
- What can you accomplish that will make reading this book worthwhile—for you, your team, and your company?
- What will you give to make this happen?
- What strengths can you apply in order to achieve these outcomes? What tendencies do you need to rein in?

 Download at thrive.shiftthework.com/accelerators

The truth of the matter is that most leaders just don't know what it takes to build a high-performance culture. This is due largely to the fact that leaders have neither an objective system for defining high performance nor an effective approach for enabling elevated levels of performance for sustained periods of time across an entire organization. If you are like most leaders, you are doing the best you can with the knowledge you have.

We know of a small company where the CEO believed reorganizing the seating chart every twelve to eighteen months was essential for success. Never, to our knowledge, did he ask for input, nor did he explain his perspective behind this belief. He simply decided when it was time to restructure—which, for him, meant "rearranging'" the physical layout. He was caught up in his own approach for making things better, and he only looked at a small aspect of the organization. Changes in the physical layout alone did not result in positive changes in business or financial results, but did adversely impact workflow, as well as office communication and collaboration.

Leaders come up with their own ways of trying to improve processes all the time, and they often assume employees will effectively implement those changes with little to no turbulence. This is a problem, but it is not a new problem. With positive intent, leaders may latch on to what they think will work, without applying the necessary rigor to assess their options and garner support for the path chosen before implementation and rollout. An example of this may be getting an idea for compensation from a peer at another company. A desired result of the compensation change (e.g., changing the mix of an individual's earnings to be more heavily weighted to incentive compensation than to salary) may be that employees are more motivated by upside earnings with the incentive component, and thus work harder, producing better results for the company. But turbulence may lie ahead. Consider:

- Have leaders run models to see how the compensation change would impact earnings?

- Have the influences on recruiting and hiring practices been considered?

- How does a move to a more incentive-laden compensation plan align with the expectations, motivations, and preferences of the impacted employee population?

Many often ignore science, research, and data because they think they know better or they just underestimate the impact of change.

In other cases, what we see is some combination of cognitive biases at play that impact decision-making and action. As an example, with the breadth and depth of data available to hiring managers, it is astounding how many companies make important hires without using analytical approaches to determine a candidate's cultural fit and true abilities or conducting quality reference checks. Having candidates take assessments and then ignoring the results, or not making use of them after the candidate is hired, provides no value. We may as well save the time and expense, as that approach is no different than not using them at all. Far too many managers make hiring decisions based on a recommendation, experience with the candidate that may not be relevant to the position in question (we often see this with internal hires, such as promoting a solid individual contributor to a manager or leader role with no evidence that the individual can lead or manage teams effectively, or at all), or gut instinct (we are all inclined to hire

 Download at thrive.shiftthework.com/accelerators

people we like). There is a conflict at play when leaders ignore important data, and this can inhibit levels of workforce performance.

Gut check: Review this list of twenty-four common biases. See which
ones filter your decision-making ability. Pick the top three that impact the way you operate and consider how you can temper those biases.

 Download at thrive.shiftthework.com/accelerators

When leaders encounter performance issues like production errors
and unattained goals, they often assume the problem lies within the employee, so they try to fix the person. They create a perfor-
mance-improvement plan or assign them to training, instead of taking a systematic approach to performance elevation. Seventy-five
percent of performance barriers are attributed to organizational factors, which are unrelated to "flaws" in the individual performers. Effective leaders can shift their perspective by looking at the entire work
system. This involves searching for barriers that impede workforce
performance, most of which have been created unintentionally, and
then employing successful change-management principles to eliminate those issues. Approaching performance systemically helps create
a positive work environment in which everyone has the potential to
operate with consistently high levels of production.

To address the truth that "fixing the person" is neither a sufficient
nor an appropriate approach to raising overall levels of performance,
we have leveraged the systematic process called the Exemplary Performance System.

CHAPTER ONE

DEFINE SUCCESS

"Would you tell me, please, which way I ought to go from here?"

"That depends a good deal on where you want to get to," said the Cat.

"I don't much care where," said Alice.

"Then it doesn't matter which way you go," said the Cat.

"so long as I get SOMEWHERE," Alice added as an explanation.

"Oh, you're sure to do that," said the Cat, "if you only walk long enough."

LEWIS CARROLL, ALICE IN WONDERLAND

Executives of a financial services company were in the process of defining high performance in specific sales roles. This initiative was prompted by a review of sales force performance data that showed unacceptable variability across the organization. Some regions performed consistently well, while others struggled. Some individuals within regions struggled, while others consistently performed well. Upon initial analysis, leaders did not see data that suggested the performance could be directly attributed to:

- Territory assignments
- Seniority in role
- Amount of training
- Raw talent
- Personal motivation

The executives had tried new hiring practices and a variety of training solutions, changed compensation programs, and replaced underperforming salespeople. Nothing they tried resulted in a material shift in performance over sustained periods of time. We had the good fortune of getting introduced to the people directly responsible for leading the sales organization, and we mutually decided that we could help crack the high-performance code with them.

When we asked each executive to list the most important quantitative and qualitative metrics of success for the sales roles, we received a range of success metrics, including:

- New sales revenue
- Total sales revenue
- Client retention
- Client relationship health
- Market penetration
- New client acquisition

The total list came to over fifteen "most important" metrics. With this lack of clarity and alignment at the executive level, you can likely see why it was so tough for the company to consistently hire, onboard, and develop high-performing people across the sales organization.

When we first meet company executives, conversations often involve asking us how we can help to improve organizational performance in some fashion (increase sales results or manager effectiveness, improve customer retention or employee engagement scores, or increase throughput in manufacturing). While these categories may ring true to you, our position is they don't provide the specificity needed to drive consistent levels of high performance. From experience, we know that when you independently ask executives the qualitative and quantitative metrics that matter most in a key business-result area (increasing sales, for example), there is significant variance in the answer from members of the same team. If executives cannot agree on the definition of what high performance looks like, their organization's struggle to have consistent high levels of performance is no surprise. The first step in the process of creating a thriving organization is defining success.

We begin this process by identifying executive leaders and key stakeholders together—those who have the most at stake in driving success across the organization. We help the leaders to agree upon and understand the initiative's objectives. They are asked to identify:

- Their most important business metrics—what success will look and feel like
- The risks of not achieving specific outcomes
- The critical roles that have the most impact on bringing the desired business results to fruition

With the critical roles identified, we conduct one-on-one meetings with the executives to get their personal view of the most important qualitative and quantitative metrics for each role. It's imperative that these conversations occur in a one-on-one fashion prior to a group discussion. When metrics conversations occur at the group level first or only, some people inevitably hold back their true thoughts, while others dominate the discussion. This creates misalignment from the outset and can kill efforts to effectively elevate performance.

Leaders often state a desired result as a high-level goal, such as achieving 30 percent revenue growth or maintaining a balanced scorecard. To more effectively define success and foster higher levels of performance, these goals must be specific and the means to attaining the goal must be communicated. For example, will growth be obtained through new business, customer retention, a mix of both, or some other way? Important goals need to be rich and full of detail. They can't be one-dimensional or vague.

New goals and strategies often are declared from the top down—an outdated and ineffective approach to this critical business process. Employees are left to figure out what these high-level targets mean for them. They receive their goals and responsibilities arbitrarily, cascaded through a performance management system, with little role context or clarity to how they can impact the organization's desired results. People want to understand why and/or how their roles matter. They simply will not put their heart and soul into something just for the money—they want a goal and a purpose.

CASE IN ACTION

A friend of ours is an economic development consultant for the state of Maryland. He recently visited a plant in Baltimore that had a large physical space with a small workforce. He had a brief meeting with the plant manager, and as the manager escorted him out, he stopped to say goodbye to an employee who was retiring—it was his last day after thirty years of service.

After thanking and congratulating this employee, he asked the employee if he had any requests before leaving. The employee said he had never been on a tour of the plant, so he wanted to walk through and see the work process from start to finish. In thirty years, he had never seen how his work impacted the big picture.

It should have been surprising that this employee was never introduced to the full work process, but unfortunately, this happens all the time. People show up to work and have no idea what the value proposition is for their role, except in a narrow and constrained way. There can be a complete disconnect between a company's strategy and purpose, and what employees experience on a day-to-day basis.

Helping an employee understand the *why* behind what she does, and the upstream and downstream relationships in a work process, creates a sense of responsibility for the individual. Accountability among coworkers is established. Understanding the *why* has a positive impact on standards of quality. When people understand a process, and their individual component of the process, their commitment to quality is renewed.

On your leadership team, who are the individuals that usually hold back?

Who dominates discussions?

What can you do to more effectively engage all leaders in important discussions and decisions to ensure their perspectives are heard and that you most effectively elevate engagement and performance?

Once goals are set, most leaders build their organizational systems and processes the way performance unfolds left to right, as shown in figure 1.1. The intent of the approach is to equip people to complete tasks that link to achievement of the organizational goals. This common approach has critical flaws that inevitably prevent sustainable growth. The better approach more successfully links business goals to higher levels of performance.

When viewing organizational performance as a system, leaders aspire to have employees exist at the center of six well-aligned arrows (influences). When this occurs, the following conditions emerge:

ROLE CLARITY

Each person in the organization has role clarity, with an understanding of how her role contributes to the goals of the entire enterprise.

FIGURE 1.1

TYPICAL APPROACH TO PERFORMANCE

SHIFT'S APPROACH TO PERFORMANCE

ACCOUNTABILITY

The awareness of each person's responsibility serves as a performance accelerator, as opposed to a weapon that results in distrust and disengagement.

ROLE-SPECIFIC, PERFORMANCE-BASED LEARNING AND DEVELOPMENT

Relevant, intentional learning, application, and coaching better enable each person to produce the most critical outputs for which she is responsible.

Where such strong alignment exists, daily tasks, accomplishments, and results support business goals. For example, in an automobile-repair business where all the arrows are aligned, a mechanic will repair a vehicle in a way that results in the satisfaction of multiple stakeholders. The specific repair will meet departmental needs (within cost and time parameters) that, in turn, support the business's financial and efficiency objectives. The work is done and communicated in ways that leave the customer feeling appreciated and valued and that link to broader organizational goals, such as customer retention, increased customer spending, and referrals.

To create this type of goal-oriented, high-performing organization, performance must be analyzed from right to left. The process for this reorientation is to:

- Establish the company purpose, vision, goals, and related metrics

- Identify the outcomes that must be produced by each part of the organization to support the goals

- With the specific desired results in mind, identify the optimal job behaviors, tasks, and actions needed to support the strategy (Note: This last piece also informs whether a role is necessary in the organization.)

WORK RIGHT TO LEFT

In some companies, money earned is the dominant measuring stick for success. "Busyness" defines worth. People take pride in pulling all-nighters, working sixteen-hour days, or swooping in at the last minute to save the day. Crisis and firefighting are the normal modes of operating.

This emphasis on activity is misguided. Putting in longer hours does not produce results that drive critical business outcomes. More-appropriate metrics that align with company strategy result in purposeful activity and performance that directly support the greater goal. When metrics don't align, the work environment is inefficient and confusing, and people become disengaged.

It's not enough to identify meaningful metrics; those metrics have to be communicated consistently. Inconsistent messages from leaders result in conflicting tasks and direction and create stress and anxiety for teams and individuals. Mindsets, behaviors, and actions can't align with company priorities when people don't know what is most important. Success must be clearly defined by leaders and threaded throughout the organization to drive higher levels of performance.

Figure 1.1 shows that high-performing leaders start in "reverse" when strategically defining roles. Instead of designing a role and defining its tasks in isolation, leaders begin by first defining outcomes, or what the role needs to produce. This provides the foundation for accelerated and amplified performance.

CASE IN ACTION

One of our clients is a well-known medical lab with hundreds of locations in the United States. They receive and analyze thousands of clinical specimens daily from many different hospitals and medical offices. Given the criticality of the work, every lab is required to have a pathologist on-site.

Working left to right, the main job responsibilities for the pathologist appeared to be entirely technical: establishing processes, quality-checking analyses, monitoring results, and providing medical expertise. This was in the initial job description, and the criteria they used to evaluate potential new hires. Had they worked right to left, they would have realized that their pathologists were also primary interfaces with clients when there were problems and clinical issues. They also supported local sales staff and served as the point of contact for new customers. The role encompassed much more than just providing clinical accuracy.

As they shifted their perspective and worked right to left, the company discovered there were multiple outcomes the pathologists needed to produce to be successful. In addition to lab experience and medical knowledge, the positions required interpersonal and problem-solving skills. They were responsible for many nonclinical tasks, so the leaders changed the hiring criteria.

Working from right to left gives you clarity around the strategic intent of a role, team, or department. It helps you determine the full range of skills, responsibilities, and tasks for each one. It will also positively impact all six influences.

IN SUMMARY

The definition of our right-to-left process and the case example out-lined above demonstrate that creating a thriving enterprise requires employees to understand how their contributions, results, and accomplishments link to the organization and its strategic intent. Without knowing the value of their performance or their role, employees have an isolated, fractured, and often uninspired view of their work.

Aligning an employee's role with the goals of the company ideally begins before she officially joins the team. Hiring managers can (and should) provide a realistic role preview during the interview process. Such a preview is designed to highlight the areas that most often attract and retain the right people as well as those aspects of the role that may cause them to fail or leave. A realistic role preview reduces the likelihood of post-hire surprises ("I didn't know I needed to do this" or "This isn't what I expected at all"). It helps a candidate understand the role and corresponding tasks and responsibilities and provides context for how the role fits into the big picture. Metrics for the job should be made clear. The candidate needs to fully understand that what she does makes a difference and that her job has an impact when it comes to achieving company goals.

Impact cuts both ways. Candidates should also understand the effects of producing substandard results. Performing poorly in their role will have some type of consequence for the enterprise. The consequence could show up as a financial loss for the company, an inconvenience to a customer, or a negative impact on a department goal. Each employee must have clarity with respect to the impact of their performance.

When leaders effectively link goals and metrics throughout the organization, it sets the stage for heightened employee engagement and for the organizational influences of the EPS to come into alignment. Making this one change facilitates significant performance acceleration through individual and organizational clarity about the impact created by what each person does and how they do it.

Think about the last time you restructured the company or modified the organizational chart. When planning the changes, did you first think about the people you have and where to put them, or did you think about the business goals you need to reach, the functional roles needed to drive those strategies, and then the people who could best fill those roles?

One of the biggest mistakes we see leaders make when doing organizational design initiatives is thinking too early about current people, as opposed to starting with the definition of business success. This leads to suboptimal performance, as leaders think about where to put people they have, instead of focusing on the needs of the business first.

ORGANIZATIONAL INFLUENCES

If you are finished changing,
you are finished.

—BENJAMIN FRANKLIN

 CHAPTER 2 ACCELERATORS

PERFORMANCE REVIEWS

BEST PRACTICES FOR EFFECTIVE 1:1 MEETINGS

We remember attending a national sales meeting for one of our clients, an event for all field sales and client retention team members, operations team members who help to deliver what the sales team sells, and senior executives from across the company. In total, over five hundred people convene annually for this important gathering. On one of the evenings, the company holds an awards ceremony, recognizing the achievements of the best sales and service team members from across the company. After an introduction by the head of sales for the company and a video montage that includes recognition and appreciation from colleagues and clients, each winner is welcomed to the stage by the CEO to say a few words of thanks and to get a photograph memorializing the achievement. From the accommodations and entertainment to the food and activities, the event is a remarkable production.

During the awards ceremony we attended, one of the senior executives shared some thoughts about what made one of the award winners so remarkable. He said things like "Clients love her; she is always there for the clients, no matter how big or small the need. She works tirelessly for our clients and company, and I often see her responding to emails and working at 3 a.m. Talk about dedication!" Our team cringed at hearing the last part of those sentiments. What may seem like a benign statement is a representation of how leaders unintentionally create barriers to higher levels of engagement and performance. In what was an opportunity to reinforce what high performance looks like and provide tangible examples of what others need to do in order to be invited to the big stage at future national sales meetings, this leader sent the message that if a person wants to be recognized as one of the best in the firm, she would need to work around the clock, sacrificing sleep, time with family, and health in unsustainable ways. Many employees left that awards ceremony questioning if the company leaders really valued them or viewed them as replaceable parts in a human assembly line.

The activity of putting a vision or mission statement on paper, or drafting a set of business strategies, goals, and tactics, will not produce a high-performing organization. Without consideration and inclusion of the three major organizational influences from the EPS—the ones that accelerate or hinder performance—leaders unnecessarily put the future of the firm at risk.

We've laid out working definitions of each of the three influences that exist in the organization and have a significant impact on the ability of each individual and team:

1. ENVIRONMENTS, SYSTEMS, AND RESOURCES:

These are external to the employee and have significant impact on engagement and performance. Examples and some questions to help explore and diagnose their utility include:

- Physical and cultural work environment—Do they foster collaboration? Stimulate curiosity and inquiry? Do they stifle energy?

- Technology systems and work processes—Are these designed with the users in mind, with an understanding of how the work is done? Or are they designed in a manner that is absent an understanding of the actual work and those who perform it?

- Tools and information—Are these easily accessible or hard to find? Are these accurate, or are they outdated? Do they align with the organization's intent to employ technology, advance digital fitness, or ensure simplicity of use?

2. EXPECTATIONS AND FEEDBACK:

As discussed in the previous section, setting clear expectations and providing context sets the foundation for consistent high levels of performance. However, merely setting expectations is insufficient—it doesn't foster and sustain high performance. Ongoing feedback can be an exponential multiplier of performance, or it can be a massive decelerator.

3. REWARDS, RECOGNITION, AND CONSEQUENCES:

These go far beyond the compensation system, and each of these plays an important role in accelerating and amplifying performance. Leaders must create and refine these in a fashion that directly aligns with organizational goals and priorities. Anything less creates confusion, frustration, disengagement, and poor performance.

While all the influences in the EPS impact performance, these first three—the organizational influences—account for 75 percent of the variance across team members and directly impact a person's ability to consistently perform at high levels.

FIGURE 2.1

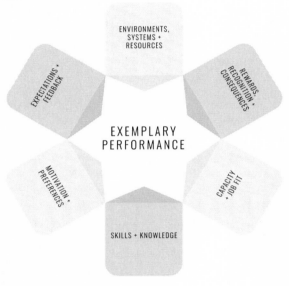

CASE IN ACTION

We worked with a company that has grown by acquisition over the past twenty years, becoming a leader in its industry. This organization started with a few locations in a couple of markets, and its founder had amazing plans for how to grow the business and transform the industry.

Each newly acquired location had its own culture, technology, systems, and processes. This company faced the challenge of meshing these individual cultures into one.

As the company grew, it held on to its small executive leadership team. As with many small organizations in their early stages, leaders made decisions and accomplished tasks simply by having casual hallway conversations. Leaders were accustomed to operating in this way, and it worked. They grew in revenue and profit, and they were in the habit of telling their people how things would be done. This company wanted to hold on to their "traditional" way of doing things—they wanted to give the acquired entities instructions from above, with no questions asked. After all, for the leaders, it was natural, it was comfortable, and it had worked up to this point.

Senior employees watched from the sidelines as the systems they were dependent on were revamped lacking a user's view, resulting in tools they found to be counterintuitive and unproductive. Corporate leaders didn't explain why changes were implemented, how employee roles linked to the changes, or why any of it mattered. Having no say in how their work was to be done, employees had to deal with inefficiencies and rework that devoured morale. They were being told how to operate and were expected to do things in a way that cost them a great deal of time and energy. They felt like second-class citizens.

The leaders believed strong sales and revenue cured all ills. The company outperformed the competition, reinforcing the leaders' belief that they knew best. All the while, people in the field were restless. In time, internal cultural issues turned into performance-related troubles and external problems.

An example of the impact of overly centralized and underinformed decision-making is how site managers' vested interest in running growing operations led them to hoard talent and hurt the company's ability to attract and retain the best people—the people it needed to grow the business. The reasons for the emergence of these outcomes included the unintended incentive site managers had to keep top employees in their markets because of how the site managers were evaluated and compensated. Site managers did not openly promote company opportunities for advancement in other markets. Given that recruiting and training replacements threatened the maintenance of their sales numbers, managers aggressively blocked their top people from growing elsewhere in the organization. This created an unwelcome reality for high-performing employees: they couldn't advance within the firm, so many left to pursue other opportunities. The company was known for lacking advancement options, so top talent shied away from applying.

To exacerbate the situation, site managers had little authority to negotiate salaries for staff and new recruits. Many were in the position of having to offer salaries that were below competitive market value. Discretionary bonuses weren't allowed either. Negotiation was not an autonomous option regardless of the amount of money involved or if the manager had the funds available in her budget. On top of that, the process of gaining corporate approval was cumbersome and painful, so the managers often chose not to engage corporate at all. Instead, they suffered in silence as their market performance fell short of expectations and potential.

Another flaw in the system was stacked rankings: one person's rising requires others to be pushed down. The culture of this company forced employees to fight for credit and attention for their achievements. Information and credit became power, causing people to warehouse or withhold information because of the advantage they perceived in doing so. A weekly sales status report assigned a value to each employee linked directly to their production. Very few found the report helpful or positive. Merely being high on the list didn't energize top producers, low producers knew they would be ostracized instead of helped, and those who fell in the middle were relieved not to be under the microscope.

There's nothing wrong with leveraging competition as part of a high-performance culture. The drive for winning can fuel business growth. However, in command-and-control operations where numbers define an employee's worth and people win only when someone else loses, competition becomes divisive and unproductive. Employees are less likely to collaborate or support one another. A staff member having a valid idea for improving the organization can make others feel threatened. When threatened, employees might respond by working back channels, undermining the credibility of the idea generator. They prioritize not being left behind over what will improve the organization.

The model this company used to measure performance had significant flaws. It couldn't provide rewards for exceptional work, because there was no true definition of what high performance looked like. This created roadblocks for talented employees—it was difficult for them to advance beyond their current positions. It also created frustration for high-potential employees, as there wasn't a clear path for advancement, nor were there resources available for development. The company culture was one of every man and woman for himself or herself and gave no consideration to the broader needs of the company.

Leaders needed to shift their perspective and find balance. They needed to hear and understand what was going on with their people. Company executives found themselves more and more distanced from their employees. Some people in leadership roles had never engaged directly with the firm's customers. The three organizational influences were massively out of alignment, making an immediate intervention imperative.

When we encounter a situation like this, we recommend using the EPS as a model for envisioning opportunities to bring about systemic and systematic change. In this specific case, we saw material improvements in clarity, alignment, and performance acceleration across the company by employing the EPS.

Let's look at the three *organizational influence* categories you need to address to realize your desire to lead or otherwise be a contributing member of an enterprise capable of and defined by high engagement and high performance.

ENVIRONMENTS, SYSTEMS, AND RESOURCES

No leader says, "I want to figure out how to make this a difficult place to work. I want to demotivate my employees. I want disengagement to wreak havoc on our company performance." These circumstances that beset too many organizations exist due simply to the lack of a model that fosters a high-performance work system. To effectively— and intentionally—influence the shape of an organization, environments, systems, and resources need to work as one.

Environments, systems, and resources are influences external to the individual contributor or team. They are determined by the organization so an individual performer can effectively do her work. These include work processes, access to resources (such as materials and information), tools ranging from apps to wrenches, and the workflows in which employees operate.

These components make work easier...or more difficult. In an ideal world, these systems and the resources to activate and sustain them are designed with the end user foremost in mind. Poorly designed and implemented elements essential to high performance result in people spending inordinate amounts of time and energy overcoming design issues and doing things that are not essential to producing key outcomes. Less-than-ideal work environments, poorly designed systems, a lack of resources, and arbitrary metrics are a few examples of factors that can create barriers to alignment. Misaligned organizational influences cause people to waste time and effort trying to connect pieces that don't fit together. This creates frustration, leads to disengagement, and can result in significant drag on financial performance.

Structures in which no one owns all the components of the performance system inherently suboptimize the system as a whole. This may be true even when each owner strives to do the right things in their respective area of responsibility. A holistic, inclusive approach to design and ownership allows everyone in the organization to contribute to operational success.

CASE IN ACTION

A call center we worked with provides a clear example of the negative impact of environmental inhibitors. In this call center, important goals included reducing the phone queues and minimizing wait times for customers. No one asked questions about how workers accomplished results that conformed with these performance standards. It turned out that the metrics unintentionally drove people to actions that didn't make sense and weren't in alignment with customer needs. Calls were transferred unnecessarily between agents because the clock "restarted" with each transfer.

We also found ergonomics was a barrier to higher levels of performance. Much of the documentation workers needed to do their jobs was filed in three-ring binders, making it difficult to find information. The work area was cramped, and computer screens were hard to see due to glare from natural light streaming through large windows. Employees sat in decrepit chairs.

The company had rewards, recognition, and consequences that were disconnected from desired business outcomes, and the physical environment inhibited optimized performance. Additionally, employees did not feel empowered to draw attention to the fact that metrics leaders used were actually negatively impacting the customer experience and driving behavior. All of this was taking a significant toll on revenue and profitability.

Improving performance wasn't just about training workers to handle calls better; it required a total redesign of the physical work environment. The solutions ranged from the simple (placing blinds on the windows) to the more complex (making workplace documentation available through the computer system). Workers had the ability to easily access the information they needed...and were able to see it! Understanding precedes action: knowing how to most effectively shift performance must start by first determining what success looks like and illuminating the barriers and accelerators linked to the desired outcomes.

As a result of employing the EPS, call center metrics were changed. Customer retention and satisfaction replaced call-handle times as the primary measures of performance, and the company saw improvement in areas of performance.

Think about your most critical business outcomes. Where and how does organizational environment play a role in preventing and accelerating performance? How do you know? Who can help you get an even better perspective of this area of impact?

POORLY DESIGNED SYSTEMS

When ATMs were first introduced, customer service representatives sat next to them to provide assistance to new users because no one knew how to use the machines yet, and the leaders of the financial institutions and the companies who built the ATMs didn't understand the customer experience. Today, we can travel all over the world, using ATMs in any language we want. Everything we need is embedded in the process and driven by automatic prompts. Similarly, tax preparation software allows people to file a return by responding to a series of questions. The program uses the answers to fill out the forms for you.

When the right performance support and job aids are embedded within a system, understanding and performance accelerate. When they are not embedded within a system, the alignment of environments, systems, and resources is inhibited, resulting in degraded business performance. We recently encountered an example of this on a poorly designed website. We went through a step-by-step process on the state of Maryland's website to find information about business taxes. At one point during the search, the website asked us to provide information that we had already entered. This lack of end-user focus is a common problem with a majority of corporate systems that we encounter. We're confident that nearly every reader of this book has experienced calling a company for information or assistance and being greeted by automated prompts to validate customer information (such as name, address, security information, and the nature of the issue). Then, when you finally are rescued from "Hold Hell," you are asked for the same information—no doubt causing frustration and a poor customer service experience. This lack of design thinking has a direct impact on critical metrics such as Net Promoter Score, revenue, customer retention, and profit.

A striking—if logical—approach to their work that we frequently observe in exceptionally high performers is their development of system shortcuts and workarounds to get what they need, despite poor design. (Note: Our use of "systems" includes business processes, not just technology systems.) Unfortunately, these high performers tend not to share these approaches with their peers. Similarly, system designers don't tap the high performers as a resource for enhancing the user interface or process design. Even in agile development environments, high performers from the end-user community are not always leveraged as a primary source of input. Shortcomings like these impede the work and negatively impact the end-user experience.

Think about your most critical business outcomes. Where and how do systems play a role in preventing and accelerating performance? How can you determine the actual impact that systems have on performance? Who can help you get an even better perspective of this area of impact?

LACK OF RESOURCES

People are the most important resource any company possesses. Helping contributors maximize the time available to do their jobs and the clarity about how their work best supports the organization's goals so they can do it well are key ingredients in the high-performance formula. Having a low enough ratio of manager to employees to ensure time and clarity are established and maintained is important in creating a high-performing organization. A low ratio by itself is insufficient to achieve this end; the managers need to be effective. A shortage of effective managers for a sales team, for example, creates constant time pressure on the managers. Lack of quality information and guidance can result in confusion about organizational goals. Activity-based metrics, such as number of sales calls, can become the key criterion used to evaluate workers. Such metrics do have merit, but the number of calls made does not reveal how many were good calls. Employees might hit a call quota but never engage customers the right way to produce the business results required of that specific role.

There is a different—and better—feeling and reality in a world where things are in order. Using the same sales team example but with an appropriate manager-to-employee ratio in place, each manager has adequate time to focus on what matters most. Plenty of the right resources are available, including an abundance of help. Conversation and observation lead to no longer measuring achievement by merely counting calls or other activities divorced from business results. Managers are able to, among other things, accompany salespeople on key client calls, helping them close more deals in real time, and tailor and actively support the development of team members over time. When we talk to members of well-aligned sales teams about one-on-one meetings with their managers, they tell us that these are a valuable use of their time. They report leaving these meetings more equipped to be successful and believe their manager has a personal interest in their growth.

Imagine how your organization would look, feel, and operate if all employees knew that their weekly one-on-one with their direct supervisor was the most impactful part of their week? When resources, including and especially managers, are properly allocated to create balanced ratios, these benefits don't have to be imagined—they exist.

Think about your most critical business outcomes. Where and how do resources play a role in preventing and accelerating performance? How do you spot resource issues? How do you or can you measure the impact of resource issues? Who can help you get an even better perspective of this area of impact?

ORGANIZATIONAL MISALIGNMENT

When operating optimally, each workplace setting or environment acts as an integrated system in support of the desired performance.

In the late 1980s, US manufacturing plants introduced greater levels of robotics and automation into their processes. At the time, assembly line employees worked in dirty plants with inventory strewn about;

groups of people stood around talking or smoking. Equipment was sometimes unreliable, and up-time was not at acceptable standards.

During this time, we took executives from a US manufacturing company to visit their counterparts at Toyota's new plant in Georgetown, Kentucky. American officials were taken aback—they would never open their doors to a competitor like this. Everything they did was considered a proprietary secret, never to be shared. But the foreign-owned company believed transparency only made it stronger and more competitive.

The American officials walked into a pristine plant; everything was stored in its proper place, and the floors were spotless. The plant had less automation and was more dependent on human workers, with every single one of them focused on the task at hand. Every line worker was empowered to stop the line if they saw a defect, either in the assembly of a vehicle or in a part they received. The workers were not only engaged in making high-quality products, they were also engaged in improving the process.

The difference between these two workplace cultures was dramatic. The US manufacturer had a culture filled with performance barriers; its workers lacked the engagement and incentives to act to make things better. The Georgetown plant, by contrast, had the right environments and systems, appropriate resources, and a commitment to creating an engaged workforce that produced highly valued deliverables. This plant was the ideal picture of organizational alignment.

EXPECTATIONS AND FEEDBACK

"I didn't know you needed that from me."

"Why didn't you tell me that earlier?"

"That's not my job."

"I've never had a performance review."

"I don't have one-on-ones with my manager."

As a leader, hearing any of these sentiments likely makes your skin crawl. Too often, these are the norms, not the exception, and you can trace many performance barriers directly to the organizational influence of setting clear expectations and providing effective feedback.

Sir Ernest Shackleton, who also famously tried to cross Antarctica on foot, provides a great example of setting clear expectations. For his expeditions, he used this language to recruit crew members:

"MEN WANTED: for hazardous journey, small wages, bitter cold, long months of complete darkness, constant danger, safe return doubtful, honor and recognition in case of success."

Shackleton consistently had droves of applicants for his journeys. Clear expectations will speak to those who believe what you believe and who share common goals. At SHIFT, we share our crusade, which you already know: to shift organizational cultures from 70 percent disengaged to 70 percent engaged. While maybe less treacherous than what Shackleton's crew experienced, we've been told that our aspirations are no less bold. At the same time, we hear that we share our mission and vision in a compelling fashion, and we consistently attract people who care about the things we hold most dear. When we recruit specifically for SHIFT Consulting, we discuss how we are, undoubtedly, the most caring, inspiring, results-driven management consulting firm on the planet. Our clients regularly ask us how we continue to add such incredible talent to our team.

During the interview process, we ask relevant questions that illuminate whether a person's passion, skills, and expertise equip her to do the required work in a way that aligns with our culture, and we offer a realistic preview of the role in a way that honestly reflects the job. When there are areas of concern about a candidate, share those concerns with the candidate. Have an open and honest conversation about your reservations and encourage the candidate to share any that she may have. This sets a solid foundation of candor and feedback that will be consistent throughout the employee's lifetime at the company. Know that this is not the norm and that candidates may need some time to fully engage in this kind of dialogue. In that candidate's mind, she may be wondering what the "right" answer is, or whether this is an interviewing tactic to get the candidate to trip up. In addition to setting appropriate expectations, you will set your company apart when operating in this fashion. There is very little, if any, chance that a new employee will be surprised by the work, or our culture, after joining SHIFT. We often see the opposite of that in many organizations. Hiring managers put on their sales hats during the interview—they want to persuade an applicant to take the job. It's all about "filling the seat." That is inefficient, at best, and stealing, at worst. Creating a situation where an employee becomes disengaged after ninety days and then quits, or worse, stays, has negative impact on morale, stress, workload, customer experience, and business results.

Leaders cannot assume that candidates with strong résumés and twenty-year track records as top producers in their field have exactly what it takes to succeed in a role within the leader's firm. To presume that the candidate will thrive immediately upon hiring shows a lack of business acumen and is irresponsible. When candidates are hired, it's important to have a sound and thorough onboarding program. Show the new hire what excellence looks like in her role and align the onboarding and training with opportunities to achieve that excellence. We call this precision hiring. Employees can't just read about performance expectations—they must be prepared, equipped, and paired with people who are already excellent in this role and can serve as models.

That same level of clarity needs to be maintained for incumbents at a company. They need to know the details of their role: what they are expected to accomplish, how they are expected to produce the desired results, how their performance will be judged, and especially, how their role adds value to the overall enterprise. Everyone deserves to know the "worth of their work." They need to see how what they do and produce contributes to the success of the enterprise.

When you hear the phrase "I'm going to give you some feedback," how do you feel? What are you expecting to follow that statement? If you are like almost every person we've met, not only are you likely bracing yourself for negative commentary about an area where you have a performance deficiency, but you are also expecting that the input will not provide value or utility. The root cause of this common occurrence lies in a lack of clarity and alignment: lack of clarity around what good performance looks like in a role, and lack of alignment around the performance metrics that matter most. Ill-equipped managers and leaders do the best they can with what they have, offering generalized input, mostly focused on what is lacking, and delivered in a fashion that often leaves direct reports uninspired, confused, and no more effective in their work than they were before the conversation with their boss.

To immediately improve in this area, consider this recipe:

- Feedback should be delivered in real time, as much as possible. The more immediate, the better.

- Better still is providing feedback with C.R.E.D.[3] in mind. The CRED system was developed by one of our managing directors, Jeff Lesher, and stands for feedback that is:

- **Constructive:** All feedback needs to be constructive. Framing it and delivering it any other way distracts from the point of feedback and can create fear, uncertainty, and doubt across the employee base.

Within a constructive framework, the nature of the feedback can and should vary, including being:

- **Reinforcing:** Make sure you provide clarity on what you value and want to see the employee do again or what does not align with culture or performance expectations, and what or how the employee needs to produce differently. ("When I heard you empathize with the customer to let him know that we understood the gravity of his issue, I knew that you had properly internalized and applied our value of empathy. Keep it up!")

- **Essential:** Feedback should tie directly to specific, role-based performance expectations and company values. Period. Anything more or less than this can become distracting.

- **Developmental:** You want to deliver feedback in a way that helps your team member get better. You can do this in a number of ways, including asking questions like "What, specifical-

---

3. Jeff Lesher, managing director, SHIFT.

ly, worked in that interaction for you? What is one thing you are going to keep doing? What is one thing you will improve next time?"

WHEN EXPECTATIONS AND FEEDBACK ARE INADEQUATE

Was it worth it?

Regardless of seniority, role, or tenure, people want to know that their contributions matter. They want to know that others see value in their work. It's more than normal to want to be valued as a member of a team. Feeling supported in and acknowledged for making progress in our work on a regular basis is on our list of wants as well. When these elements of reinforcement and development are experienced, we call this doing meaningful work—work that matters.

The sad reality, though, is that most people don't experience this. They don't know if their work matters. Do their bosses value their contributions? They have no way to measure whether what they did on a given day was worth it. When friends and family ask how their day was, most people say things like "Another day, another dollar" or "Same stuff, different day." The Lewis Carroll quote "If you don't know where you are going, any road will get you there" applies...with a destination of uncertainty or a sense of disappointment resulting from a lack of clear expectations.

The solution is not found in job descriptions. Many people have some version of a job description, though most are poorly constructed. Job descriptions tend to be lists of tasks to be done and the general skills and competencies to do them, but they lack the clarity of what the organization really needs from this role to drive business success (more on this later, when we talk about role excellence). The absence of a sense of purpose leaves people to meander through their day, performing tasks without an understanding of how what they're doing connects to the overall business goals. This disconnection leads to disengagement and substandard performance.

To test whether these things are true in your company, consider the last new hire you brought into the organization. How did you make clear to her the value she needs to produce in her role? How did you connect her specific contributions to your organization's strategies and value chain? Using your most recent team meeting as a barometer, will every employee we poll say that their time was of high value? Our experience allows us to conclude with confidence that the majority of employees will not answer in the affirmative. We're equally confident that a wandering, dispirited, and underperforming workforce is not the vision you have for your company. We know you can do better.

Think about:

- Your last new hire
- The last meeting you led
- Your work yesterday

As you consider each, ask yourself—was it worth it? If yes, what made it so? If no, what will you do make that same or a similar event worth it next time, and every time from now on? How will you more effectively invite others to engage in ways that will make the interactions worth it for them? After all, every person who is present in an interaction shares responsibility for making that interaction productive.

INEFFECTIVE ONE-ON-ONE MEETINGS

You need a positioning of one-on-ones. We've laid out the importance of being clear about the purpose of our roles and how we create value through the work we do in those roles. Of the tools available to us as people responsible for contributing through others, one-on-one conversations can be among the most impactful. Unfortunately, when it comes to meetings of any kind, quality use of that time tends to fall well short of its possibilities.

In our interactions with tens of thousands of employees, the clear majority express a common feeling: one-on-ones are not a productive use of their time—some even perceive them to be obstacles to higher levels of engagement and performance. Research shows that there are as many as eleven million meetings every day in the United States, with employees spending up to ten hours of their week either in or preparing for those meetings. Microsoft has shared their self-analysis/manager misery index that concluded that the more meeting hours per week, the more miserable the manager. Across many companies, managers spend almost 40 percent of their time in meetings, according to a Bain & Company study, with upper-level executives spending as much as 50 percent.

In general, organizations do a poor job of meeting management. We define meeting management as setting a clear purpose for the meeting, being precise in who needs to attend the meeting, preparing for and executing the meeting, and then setting productive accountabilities in place following the meeting (e.g., we go do what we said we would). Based on our research and our experience in working with over seven hundred businesses, one-on-one meetings—as conducted in most organizations—are just another time-wasting event. Why? Because they:

- Lack purpose
- Lack appropriate ownership (The employee should own the agenda and content, not the manager.)
- Lack proper preparation
- Lack follow-up

According to the thousands of employees we've surveyed, these meetings—when they do occur—are more a "check the box" activity in which the manager talks at the employee, telling her where to focus, what to do, and likely running through a tactical list of tasks and how those should be addressed. There is good news. Better leveraging one-on-one meetings to better align organizational influences is something we all can do. When organizational influences are properly aligned, attitudes shift. One-on-ones become some of the most valuable times in a manager's and their team members' week, and they have a positive impact on engagement and performance. Here is how you can make this happen.

One-on-one meetings are principally about employees' development, and they're a time for the employee to talk about their most critical goals and their progress toward those desired outcomes. These sessions are most effective when the employee—not the manager—drives the agenda and leads the conversation.

When addressing goals, progress, and outcomes, the manager should practice active listening and use the points discussed to emphasize and—where necessary—draw the employee's attention to what is most important: how their objectives, efforts, and progress relate to excellence in the role and to the employee's mutually agreed upon annual performance goals. The one-on-one is a productive forum in which to raise and discuss barriers to progress, with the manager responsible for joining with the employee to overcome those barriers.

The support of the employee's development can be addressed from many angles. For example, is the employee ready to hit the next level of certification in her role? Does he want to become a manager or team leader? Is the employee progressing toward her learning goals? A manager should invite a focused update with a prompt like "Catch me up on what actions you've taken to [address a specific area of need or opportunity] since our last conversation?" "How would you assess your progress—did you do [the thing] better? Did better things happen? Please be specific." "What did doing this feel like?" "Where have you fallen down or experienced backsliding?" "What barriers are you encountering?" On this point, helping to distinguish between externally created barriers and those arising from the stories we tell ourselves is important. Managers should ask about how they can assist—"What do you need from me?"—and step in with proactive guidance, such as "Something I've done or seen work in similar situations..." if their team member is stuck or in uncharted waters, experientially. This dialogue should feel like a mental CrossFit workout. We call this Precision Coaching.

VAGUE FEEDBACK

We once talked to an employee who said, "My boss told me I didn't get the promotion because I'm not a good team player." When the employee asked what that meant, her boss said, "Well, you need to work better with your colleagues." That feedback was not helpful; the employee had no idea how to interpret it or what to do with it to improve. She thought of herself as a good team player—she thought she had strong relationships with colleagues. She had no idea what she should do to improve performance in the specific area where she was deficient. In the moment, she was ill-equipped to take the conversation further to get more clarity. She left the meeting uninspired, confused, and feeling undervalued.

Managers can turn these development opportunities from demoralizing to hopeful and even energizing by using the CRED model we described earlier. You might say something like "I know you're working on developing deeper client relationships to help us expand our business and the lifetime value of our customers. In the past month, there are two examples of you doing this well that I've seen." Follow that with a highlight reel of what you saw: actions they took directly, how they involved others, what you saw happen as a result...anything you want them to keep doing and do more of is appropriate to reference. Remember: this process is important because it helps people do good, not merely feel good.

Managers also must provide specific feedback about opportunities for development (adding something, doing more of something, doing something with more confidence) and those essential areas requiring improvement. An essential item most often is a behavior that does not align with the organization's values, its vision, and/or their individual goals. These gaps or problematic actions need to be specifically addressed as soon as they're observed. Note: It is not necessary to include every element of development—what we want to keep seeing, what else we'd like to see, and something that needs to stop or change—in every conversation. In fact, reinforcement of what you value most can stand alone and carry far greater weight if it's absent of "but" or "however." The address of things that otherwise are precluding someone's success can be tied to something they do well to provide an example they can build on or at least a reason for optimism. Rewiring our approach to break free of the flawed formulaic belief that we need to hide criticism inside of praise—as though we're giving a pill to a pet—is one of the outcomes we wrote this book to help you achieve.

Coupled with specificity, timeliness is key to feedback's effectiveness. The days of having an annual performance review as the only performance-based conversation should be long gone (although we still see many companies who employ this practice). At SHIFT, we've consistently applied the discipline of weekly one-on-ones with our team members. Those discussions link directly to each person's OKRs (objectives and key results). We use an online platform called 15Five (www.15five.com) as a way to foster tight alignment between our contributors and their direct supervisors. The weekly updates each member of our team provides through the system inform whatever conversations they have and provide a pulse of the company to our leadership team. This flow of information ensures that our people maintain a primary focus on their priorities. This system of performance management also creates space for conversation about alignment and to provide and receive feedback on a regular basis (no less frequently than weekly). Our people are representative of the workforce overall: they have such an insatiable thirst for and actively seek input from peers and their direct supervisor about how they can constantly evolve and consistently get even better at what they do and what they want to do next. Regardless of the platform you use, you can create the same environment!

 Download at thrive.shiftthework.com/accelerators

CONTRADICTORY INFORMATION

For managers to be effective in guiding their teams to what matters most, it's important that they have been provided with a clear picture of expectations their leaders have of them. These expectations should include how the manager should be supporting her team. Whatever example leaders set likely ignites a chain reaction of similar behavior throughout the organization. Here's an example to illustrate this point, using the call center criteria we referenced previously:

Some senior managers were telling frontline managers to get their teams to "just get calls done!" Executive leadership, however, had told the frontline managers that the company's desired outcomes were to create more high-performing direct reports and grow team capabilities. Frontline managers had a choice to make: whether to ask for clarification, requiring the synchronization of two levels of leadership and risking seeming to call out their direct supervisors. In a healthy, productive environment, the frontline managers should feel and exercise the license to say to their direct supervisors, "Hey, my understanding is that we're looking to do things in ways that raise our team's capabilities. I'm having trouble aligning 'get calls done' with our organizational value of continuous improvement. Your help in resolving this conflict is appreciated."

Environmental pressures or lack of alignment can occur at any time. Everything can be humming along in an organization—clarity and alignment exist; people have a line of sight into how their work is driving results. Then, the company has a bad quarter. Just like that, reactive measures get instituted: new work processes, new incentives (such as a sales contest), workforce reductions, and emphasis on and measurement of activities that may not align with desired outcomes that remain in place. The new wrinkles muddy what was previously clear, and the company adopts practices that degrade performance.

LACK OF CAREER MOBILITY

Anyone willing and able to demonstrate high performance wants to grow and evolve in their work, but not everyone wants to vertically ascend in an organization to become a manager or leader. Growth and development look different for each person. Many want to be great individual contributors. Leaders need to understand that what moves people is far more complex than a linear path to new job titles and higher pay. We regularly encounter executives who believe, for example, that any salesperson worth her salt is motivated by money, brought to action like a coin-operated machine. Data and research do not support this notion.

In high-performance cultures, leaders understand that the reality of motivation is far more nuanced. During the hiring process, these leaders may provide offer letters that include a preview of what two-, three-, and five-year career paths might look like. In these cultures, a definitive path is not carved in stone nor necessarily linear. Career and growth expectations and desires are part of a mutual dialogue from the beginning of the relationship between employee and manager. Growth and mobility, including advancement opportunities, are part of an open, ongoing dialogue.

When career-aspiration conversations don't happen, employees leave. One of the more powerful questions that recognizes this and flags this issue is "In the last six months, has someone at work talked to you about your progress?" There is a shared responsibility for having these discussions of interest and possibility. Rather than bringing the matter out in the open with their team members, employers tell us the employee should own this issue. Employees, meanwhile, say it's a leadership duty to clearly present these opportunities. To break this passive-aggressive cycle, successful companies build a dynamic of open exploration and expectation-setting. This allows career paths and options to be embedded into the structure of an organization.

In large organizations, employees must be able to navigate complex matrices—it's a critical skill. Organizational charts do not reveal how to thrive in a matrixed environment. Leaders seeking to support their team members' aspirations must be organizationally agile and able to identify where influence and subject-matter expertise lies and whom they can tap to provide quality mentorship. When development is supported well, organizational navigation is discussed frequently. Career paths won't unfold by luck or accident for most people. Occasionally, it's the organization that gets lucky, like it did with Danielle, a former leadership student in a class we taught at a local university.

Danielle works for a prestigious healthcare system in the Baltimore area. She was inspired by what we covered in class and the idea of leading more effectively. She took the initiative to attend an event that recognized women who excel in their careers. While she was there, she bumped into the new CEO of her organization.

The CEO expressed surprise at seeing Danielle, whom she'd met just once before in passing. She asked if Danielle had used a company-sponsored ticket for the event. Danielle was unaware of the company tickets; she'd paid her own way. This impressed the CEO, and she encouraged Danielle to apply to a prestigious leadership development program inside their organization.

Danielle talked to her boss afterward, who didn't know about the internal leadership program. They did some research together and found out it was tough to get into—one of the toughest programs for an aspiring leader to gain admission to. Other colleagues told Danielle it was competitive; they had been rejected two or three times. Danielle decided to take a chance, and she was accepted into the program.

Danielle learned that this renowned institution has leadership development and career progression tracks that are not made obvious to everyone within the organization. Those who did know about them viewed them as difficult or impossible to get into. Her organization recognized they were not doing well in this area, and the new CEO is working to change performance-development and career-path programs.

REWARDS, RECOGNITION, AND CONSEQUENCES

When it comes to rewards, recognition, and consequences, we often see the confirmation bias at play with leaders. They bring existing beliefs about what they think or have experienced as motivating and being most important to employees and apply that thinking to everyone. This approach results in unintentionally created misalignment in their organizational performance systems. Despite the data about compensation and overall rewards and recognitions, some leaders still think that compensation is the only thing people are concerned about when taking or keeping a job. While money is a factor, other factors play an equal or greater role in attracting and retaining top talent. Base salary and other financial remuneration tend to be "satisfiers," essentially basic expectations—the price of admission, so to speak. That's why rewards, recognition, and consequences must stretch beyond pay alone and include elements like project assignment, work tools, conference attendance, subsidized transportation, and much more. By identifying and providing access to "motivators" that are revealed as your team's drivers, you will much more effectively inspire higher levels of contribution and productive retention for groups of employees and individuals. These insights can be gleaned through everything from market research to one-on-one dialogues.

UNBALANCED COMPENSATION SYSTEMS

Organizations can have arbitrary or unbalanced compensation systems. For example, companies have two primary sales targets: new customers and the retention and expansion of relationships and business with current customers. Consequently, sales teams historically have two types of people: those who need to find new business and those with a primary focus of maintaining and growing existing business. To be successful in the new business role, we need people who love the thrill of the exploration of new opportunities: meeting new people, unearthing new opportunities, and racking up new wins for themselves and the company. The latter group loves—and benefits from—working with existing customers and deepening those relationships, ensuring that current and future solutions demonstrably help customers to achieve their goals.

For each role to deliver significant economic value to an organization, appropriate recognition and rewards are needed. A compensation structure that awards a higher percentage of commissions to the acquisition of new business aligns more with the first role—providing more incentive to bring new customers through the door. The employees who thrive by deepening relationships and retaining customers will not thrive with the same compensation system—nor will we drive the behaviors needed to access that part of our market. We worked with a financial services client whose teams comprise externally and internally focused salespeople. One of the factors that created significant drag in their performance system was the misalignment of compensation. Each person operated in her own self-interest, and it resulted in a lack of team cohesion, increased stress, lost productivity, and an inconsistent client experience.

Teams that combine externally and internally focused salespeople add complexity to designing a well-aligned, high-performing system. Creating an environment in which we know what it looks like when the team wins and a team member understands the value her role brings and how she receives value by creating value (aka how she earns) takes time, analysis, understanding, and careful consideration.

This may seem intuitive, but too many organizations fail to focus on the purpose of the role, the value the role needs to deliver, and the people best equipped to deliver that value, and to align rewards and recognition to encourage and accelerate those results.

DECELERATION THROUGH RECOGNITION

Recognition can take many forms—it doesn't always have to take the form of money. We did work with Yum! Brands, the company that operates Kentucky Fried Chicken, Pizza Hut, and Taco Bell restaurants. We happened to be at the corporate headquarters—a large open space—on a day when somebody did something exceptional. Suddenly, an all-employee band walked in, armed with drums and kazoos, and launched a celebration for the person responsible for the big accomplishment.

This marching-band scenario would fall flat with 90 percent of our clients, but their cultures might get traction from balloons or flower deliveries as recognition. Other managers might hand out gift certificates to restaurants or to the movies; the monetary value doesn't have to be high. The goal is to ensure that people have clarity about what the organization values and that they play a critical role in moving us toward our desired goals and outcomes. By recognizing them when they do something that aligns with what delivers value, we effectively reinforce that behavior and invite more of it. Our awareness of the efforts we seek to recognize needs to transcend physical proximity. As more and more people now work part of their time outside of businesses' physical space and our teams include 1099ers, leaders need to think about how to include the entirety of their workforce in their efforts to meaningfully engage them.

Leaders must be wary of unintentionally having recognition be experienced as a negative consequence—actually making visible achievement something to avoid. Here's how this unintended demotivation can occur: high performers excel, leaders place those individuals on committees, assign special client projects, or ask them to design new solutions. This happens because leaders see value and further potential in these individuals. They know they can rely on them to deliver value. Leaders imagine this access to decision-making or influence as a perk. We say "imagine" because there often is little or no conversation with the "awardee" about these assignments. It's not malicious, but it is lazy. This sort of recognition seeks additional contribution on top of existing work and can result in fifty-five- and sixty-hour workweeks. Being the go-to person can be seductive at first, seen by employees as a growth opportunity. When they're tapped over and over, the shine of this additional work fades, and many will end up feeling resentful—that other employees are not stepping up and that they have an unsustainable workload. The very skills and enthusiasm that created the opportunities can atrophy as those "muscles" are overused. Their level of success diminishes, and they end up in what we sometimes call "day jail"; a place they neither desire to enter nor desire to remain. The net effect of actions taken to reinforce desired and desirable behavior can be that we figuratively kill off the very talent we wanted to nurture.

Moving from unintended consequences to negative reinforcement, rewarding high levels of production that occur due to bad organizational behavior is a practice leaders can fall into when they don't check under the operational hood to understand the success of someone with a reputation for "getting things done." Sustainable high performance is not supported by an "ends justify the means" environment. If the production being lauded comes through someone, for example, being verbally abusive to others, you may be dealing with a cultural cancer. In many organizations, and for most people, this sort of behavior does not align in any way to the company's values. However, because the person produces at high levels, this behavior gets swept under the rug. This sends a very dangerous message to the rest of the company about what really matters most. The message helps the cancer metastasize. For some, they take it as a cue to be similarly disrespectful to their colleagues. Others shut down and leave. In a world where the inability to find enough of the right people to fuel their organization is at the top of most executives' lists of what keeps them up at night, it's important to remember this when you tolerate corrosive behavior: those who can leave, do. (Read: You're driving away your best people.)

CASE IN ACTION

An SVP at one of our clients was known for getting results. He took immense pride in being ranked number one and in being recognized as a leader. He was often lauded for his tenure with the firm, and his rigorous tracking and follow-up on key revenue metrics. If there was a product or service that the firm sold, he had a tracker for it. He was also known for leadership tactics that resulted in his direct reports and other team members feeling belittled or dehumanized when performance was not to his standards. Many people felt like nothing they did was ever good enough. Some members of his team commented that they needed to allow for 50 percent of their week for the fire drills that this leader caused, time that directly pulled them away from producing higher levels of results. Tolerating, and even applauding, this kind of leadership behavior sent mixed messages to the rest of the organization, often causing employees to question how serious executives were about having a winning culture and what behavior was not only condoned but also rewarded.

A CLIMATE OF INJUSTICE

We know a manager who is counseling a young, exceptional achiever within his company. He's only been there for about eighteen months, and in that short time, the scope of his role has expanded dramatically. He routinely gives presentations at C-level meetings and is asked to provide feedback to various teams. He's been promised both a promotion and a salary increase for the past six months, yet it keeps getting postponed. His boss recently left for another position, so the new supervisor needs to reintroduce the promotion and shuttle it through the system—again.

While this unfolds, the employee continues to love his work; he is well compensated, and he is dedicated. Still, an unfulfilled promise hangs over everything—he lacks clarity about how recognition and rewards work, and his leaders are not following through on their commitments to him. This is a climate of injustice. Fortunately, for this employee, the climate changed.

We can report that, as part of his progression, he was given the lead on a major company initiative. Sometimes he finds himself working three sixteen-hour days in a row at special events. His manager understands the impact of his employee working these events. Wanting to provide a reward that would be most welcome and helpful, the manager took into account that the employee has a toddler with whom he never spends enough time. They agreed on the reward being additional time off. Aligning rewards with an employee's preferences increases its value. There are other employees who, given the same choice, would have opted for compensation.

This example raises the issue of fairness, transparency, and caring. Fairness doesn't mean equity—not everyone is or should be at the same point in the compensation schedule or growth cycle. People need to have the sense that the company handles rewards honorably, doing what they say they will and what reasonable people think is right. This sense is established by making sure people have information that builds their understanding of how things work when it comes to triggering consideration of recognition and rewards. We're talking here about criteria for promotions and how to get invited to take on stretch assignments. Transparency illuminates process and options—not a one-size-fits-all address to every circumstance.

IN SUMMARY

The three organizational influences discussed in this chapter—Environments, Systems, and Resources; Expectations and Feedback; and Rewards, Recognition, and Consequences—align to comprise overall corporate culture. For organizations to thrive, their people need to thrive. Systems design and integration should start with the vision and strategy of the company, establishing clarity and helping to maintain alignment among the top layers of leadership. Leaders then can effectively align the three influences and keep them in sync directly and, ultimately, through everyone else throughout the organization.

This cascade of influence and accountability is driven by the behavior modeled by senior leadership for the divisional, departmental, team, and individual levels. Beyond modeling, there is the activation of a culture of inquiry in which regular probing occurs on processes like feedback and compensation. Questions that should be asked include "Are we being true to our strategy and vision? Are the pieces coming together in ways that create a supportive and barrier-free work setting for our people?"

Curiosity and the inquiry that flows from it feed transparency. An employee must understand expectations and how he fits into the broader work system, and be able to answer questions like "What are the handoffs?" "What are the impacts of doing my job well?" "What are the consequences of operating at a substandard level?" and "How does the system provide rewards and recognition for individual and team performance?"

A well-aligned organization consistently provides clear overall expectations and consistent and meaningful feedback for all levels of employees—from executives to those on the front line. Expectations align with company goals, and feedback is specific. Goal setting, check-ins, mile markers, and one-on-ones occur in a steady, constant stream. Comprehensive performance reviews are held annually. There are various career advancement options. Opportunities are shared and explored regularly.

We implore organizations to design and implement systems and processes that transform their work environments into ecosystems that enable and encourage their people to work in ways that produce better business results. New hires should feel inspired by their company's vision, understand the expectations for their roles, and receive ongoing feedback about how they're doing in the frame of those expectations. High-performing employees need to have the necessary resources, processes, and tools available to support them.

When individual contributors, line managers, and directors are able to see how the pieces of the puzzle fit together, the magic of high performance is enabled. Cross-departmental understanding of how one person's work relates to another's creates a camaraderie and cohesion that supports better outcomes and better experiences. Whenever and wherever behavior consistent with the expressed preferences of the company occurs, recognition by direct supervisors and others, through appropriate rewards, earns more of the same and better from its people.

This is the essence of purpose-driven organizations—the kind we help grow and sustain. To create a whole that is greater than the sum of its parts where those parts don't compete but complement one another is the outcome we help create through a thriving, well-aligned organization.

INDIVIDUAL PERFORMANCE

Great performance is more valuable than ever. But where does it come from?

GEOFF COLVIN, TALENT IS OVERRATED

 **CHAPTER 3 ACCELERATORS**

Charles was the first person that executives recommended we study in our effort to define high performance in our client's regional vice president role. He was, they said, far and away their best performer, and they wanted to understand why and how he consistently outperformed his peers. When we asked the executives for their hypotheses as to why Charles consistently performed at such high levels, they said things like:

- He worked harder than most, often starting early and working into the evenings.
- He had good relationships with his clients.
- He had deep product expertise and industry knowledge.
- He had a good territory.

While the factors to which executives attributed Charles's success were in place, they were not what led to his success. In fact, there were many people across the organization who had the same role and also got up early and worked late, had good relationships, deep product and industry knowledge, and good territories, yet did not achieve the levels of success that Charles did. The company executives were perplexed by this and viewed solving this mystery as a critical factor in successfully growing their business.

When we studied Charles by interviewing him and shadowing him through the entirety of his day, we uncovered critical insights that helped to decode some of the secrets to his success. For example, while Charles did work hard, he applied his hard work in the context of his personal motivations, and how those motivations aligned with the purpose of his job. He started each day with a focus of serving his clients with solutions that would help them fulfill their mission and goals as a way to ensure his family was able to live a lifestyle that aligned with their personal vision and values. That important nuance was the difference between just working long hours and being intentional in preparation, thoughtful in every client and prospective client connection, and resilient in the face of adversity. Charles found ways to work around organizational inefficiencies and barriers that frustrated average performers. He found ways to create more time in his day to improve his output. One profound example of this innovation was that Charles hired a personal driver to take him to appointments every day, so he could increase his focused time on the phone with prospects and

clients. This one investment allowed him to make more quality client connections, resolve client issues in a more timely fashion, and quickly make new appointments if his schedule changed.

Think about the individuals in your organization who consistently outperform others. What is it that they bring to their work that others lack? Looking past what they do, to better understand why and how they do what they do, will give you clues for solving the mystery of high performance in your organization.

In 1997, a new idea arose from McKinsey & Company's Steven Hankin, which is called "the war for talent."[4] In 2001, the book The War for Talent was published. The basic premise was that the success of a company hinged on hiring and retaining people with the greatest amount of raw talent. This attribute was never fully defined, although the preface notes, "A certain part of talent eludes description: You simply know it when you see it." While the book and its premise are dated, the philosophy of hiring based on raw talent remains pervasive.

Portions of the classical HR function soon became the "talent management" organization charged with recruiting, developing, and retaining talented, "high potential" employees. This became a widely accepted trend, and organizations began encouraging managers to recruit candidates whose skills exceeded the level required for any specific job. The fear was that, if exceptional talent wasn't grabbed when it was available, it would be unavailable when a company needed it most. The focus in recruiting shifted from one's demonstrated competency to her potential. The belief was that people with high levels of potential—the capacity to do well—would inevitably perform at high levels. This bet was made on people irrespective of their fit with the immediate job or when it came to fit with the work culture or environment. The dominant theme for human resources and talent management leaders was that people with raw talent would be able to successfully take on any role within a company.

4. Ed Michaels, Helen Handfield-Jones, and Beth Axelrod, The War for Talent (Boston: Harvard Business Press, 2001).

The evidence does not support this belief. Simply possessing talent or potential does not equate to consistent high levels of performance. There is no proof that people with raw talent can fill all roles equally well.

Our research and experience lead us to conclude that individuals bring three significant performance accelerators to an organization (represented by the bottom three arrows in the EPS). They are always role-specific and context-sensitive! Here is a brief description of each:

CAPACITY AND JOB FIT

During the hiring process and when considering career progression, leaders must understand and relate a person's abilities (today and in the future) and job fit to the organization's needs. Too often, leaders either look at the people on their team and try to find places for them or take high-performing individual contributors and promote those individuals to a management role. Both are flawed approaches to organizational design. Instead, leaders need to begin analyzing the critical functions needed to execute their organization's strategies. Leaders then are able to identify the people who can most consistently perform those functions with high levels of proficiency.

SKILLS AND KNOWLEDGE

Using the right-to-left analysis approach we outlined earlier, the skills and knowledge sought in candidates should align directly with the most critical outputs required for a specific role. Learning, development, and training should support only what is most important for the role. We call this a "lean approach to learning and performance." Anything that falls outside of those parameters may distract or disengage employees, and thereby waste company resources.

MOTIVATIONS AND PREFERENCES

Much like with capacity and job fit, leaders need to understand the value systems of candidates during the hiring process. What is most important to them? Why do they do the things they do? What were the conditions present when they previously were at their very best? We strongly recommend using diagnostics and data to better understand each potential new hire. Hiring a person whose values and drivers don't align with the firm's will come back to haunt all parties involved, without exception.

A major hotel chain had long used revenue management as a key competitive differentiator. They hired revenue managers based on a strong "talent" in mathematics and numerical analysis. They trusted they would be good analysts who could impact the hotel properties' decisions on pricing. Managers banked on the idea that if they corralled talented people, their company would benefit immediately.

This hiring approach ignored the fact that initial capacity (talent) does not determine a person's level of performance. While these "highly capable" mathematicians could crank out accurate data, the desired impact on profitability of the hotel properties was highly inconsistent. Analytical talent alone was not producing the desired results, nor was the accuracy of the data. It turned out that the probability of the individual properties benefiting from the analysis was dependent on the relationship the revenue manager developed with the property management team. Many of the most talented folks produced accurate recommendations that were never used by the property management team. These analysts simply delivered "the" answer and assumed it would be implemented because it was "correct."

This case study is similar to the example of the major biomedical laboratory company from chapter 1 where pathologists were hired based upon their clinical expertise. The assumption was that their clinical expertise somehow translated into being good lab managers. It turns out that significant interpersonal and problem-solving skills were required for success in the job.

When leaders lack clarity about results (primary accomplishments), or the qualitative and quantitative metrics of success for a specific role, there are negative impacts on the organization and its people. Bad personnel decisions (hiring, career-pathing, promotions, and so forth), lost revenue opportunities (new business and existing customer growth), process inefficiencies, and disengagement are just a few of those impacts. The lack of clarity can flow from as well as feed into limited and self-defeating hiring approaches, like "I'm going to hire based on résumés" or, in the case of sales, "I'm just going to look at how much business was sold in the past." Raw skills and past accomplishments are necessary criteria to evaluate, but they are insufficient in predicting future performance.

Let's look at each of these components in more depth.

CAPACITY AND JOB FIT

When we think about role capacity, we often think about IQ and not enough about EQ (emotional quotient). Take a moment to consider your organization's hiring practices. Do you hire based solely on résumés, or do you look at organizational goals and ensure the EPS components are properly aligned? What cognitive biases may be at play during selection and hiring? For example, we often see the framing, halo, and confirmation biases adversely impact hiring precision. Are accountability measures in place? Are there explicit requirements for people to succeed in a role? When properly identified, do you use these requirements to inform employee selection? Requirements should include values and behaviors, along with production numbers. If you don't know what "good" looks like—measures of success—a persuasive but less-than-ideal candidate might more easily sway you. Without the rigor and accompanying protection of legitimate requirements of the job, people inherently hire others whom they connect with, like, or see themselves in.

CASE IN ACTION

A new salesman was hired at an accounting and finance firm, based on the recommendation of an outside consultant. He was given a salary of $210,000 plus commission—double what his coworkers made—based on his exceptional résumé. After nine months, this new hire had sold nothing and had no qualified potential business opportunities in his pipeline. During his performance review, he used his amazing sales ability to negotiate a raise. Yes, you read that right—a RAISE! A few months later, a new supervisor became responsible for this salesperson's performance. He determined that he was not meeting performance expectations, and he fired him. Think about the negative impact that occurred over the course of the year: the potential brand erosion, the existing-customer impact (due to a poor service experience), lost opportunities, and the deterioration of morale inside the company for overpaying and keeping such a poor performer. This may seem like an exaggerated hypothetical, but unfortunately, this is a true story.

The point here for your consideration and action is to focus on a person's ability to appropriately and effectively apply his talent in a way that will help you advance your business goals. A generalized skill that is not aligned with your business context provides zero value to your firm.

For capacity and job fit, look for alignment between what an individual brings to the table and the specific role you need to fill. Some requirements are concrete. In the case of a package courier, for example, a candidate may need to be able to lift a seventy-five-pound box a certain height and do so a given number of times in a day to qualify for the job. That's a defined need with clear capacity implications that can be easily measured. At the same time, while that defined need may create an unconscious bias toward "physically hulky men," it may not always yield the best candidate. For example, for couriers to thrive throughout an entire day, they will need to work successfully without injury (sustainability)—someone less bulky and truly more "fit" may be better.

We'd like to say managers don't let physical appearance influence hiring practices, but they do. A classic (and offensive) bias survived for years in the pharmaceutical industry: the preference for hiring former cheerleaders. Since part of the sales representative's job is to get face time with doctors, it was thought that physical appearance could be used to gain an advantage. Several narrow assumptions drove this sales representative profile, among them that most doctors are male, most cheerleaders are female, and the former cheerleaders tend to be attractive.

In many organizations, assumptions have significant influence on what capabilities hiring managers think people bring to the table. Remember the poor-performing sales representative who managed to get a raise? He was exceptionally charming and worked that charm to get what he wanted. In sales, there tends to be a personality bias. There is a misconception that introverts cannot thrive in a sales role. Our research and experience indicate that the abilities to produce cogent, meaningful analyses of a territory and to produce a consistently healthy pipeline of potential customers are key to high-performing salespeople and accurate predictors of their long-term success. They are *not* dependent on "charm."

Companies need to identify what is required for a role and hire people who can do the work consistently and with high levels of proficiency. Establishing rigorous parameters helps to eliminate cultural biases and increase hiring precision.

CAPACITY AND JOB FIT: INHIBITORS TO SUCCESS

Organizations must have defensible selection criteria; judgments about capabilities can't be made in an arbitrary or capricious way. That defensibility is as important internally as externally. We want to be able to answer questions about why we hired someone and be able to consistently replicate our success. The example of the courier reminds us it's easy to check for a valid driver's license, and it's easy to see if a candidate can pick up a heavy box. However, we want to avoid looking at a candidate and thinking, "I doubt she has a driver's license" or "I bet he can't lift that box."

In order to best select high performers, it's not enough to focus on candidates who just meet basic job requirements, such as having a history of specific and consistent success in surpassing leading and lagging indicators similar to those needed in your role. Candidates also need to show the demonstrated ability to learn, adapt, overcome obstacles, think creatively, and win. Lofty? Not if your aim is to build a thriving organization. To realize that entirely reasonable objective, you have to put the people with the right performance DNA into a performance-tuned environment. The selection process is the setting in which, and the time to determine, if you have the right match. A résumé may provide indicators of possible success with a new organization (such as an increase in sales over time). To determine if someone can truly perform at high levels in the specific role, hiring managers must ask specific questions in an interview and probe for sufficient detail. You might never know, for example, if the increased sales production they cite resulted from specific things the individual did or factors external to her, such as an expanded territory or client-related factors, like an acquisition that necessitated more products from the salesperson's company.

 Download at thrive.shiftthework.com/accelerators

When hiring to fill a customer service position, customer focus is an important behavior. To explore a candidate's demonstrated ability in and capacity for this pivotal area of performance, hiring managers need to orient questions to elicit specific and tangible evidence. If a candidate says she is good at and enjoys dealing with customers, many interviewers leap to the conclusion that the person is a good match. In fact, among your considerations should be whether she deals with them effectively and in a way that aligns with your specific business goals. Being more precise in the interview process allows you to seamlessly test for alignment. Ask something like "Tell me about a time when you over-delivered for a client" or "Tell me how you determine the appropriate level of customer service. What's your favorite example of doing this? What were the most impactful results of this effort?" The door is now open to a level of understanding the candidate. How does the person distinguish between customer-related situations? Do they believe that quick response time is the most positive measure of customer service? If so, she could put some of your most critical customer relationships at risk by deprioritizing working on a service issue for a $500,000 customer when a $5,000 customer calls with an issue that is important to them. A decision matrix counter to yours—one that emphasizes solving the most recent or the least time-consuming issue—could create a big issue for your company.

Résumés are designed to be brag sheets, offering clues, not answers. The increasing use of technology to cull out the "right" résumés likely is exacerbating our belief that we know more than we do about the candidate's abilities to meet your needs. We need to use our opportunities to interact with prospective team members to get much closer to knowing their entire work-relevant story. When you're clear about what is most important for success in a specific role, you can effectively probe for predictive indicators—those qualitative and quantitative metrics your highest performers use to make adjustments to their work in order to get the best results—by far. Laziness in the hiring process and failure to do your homework about the role and then the candidates cements your fate: you will make hiring mistakes you could have avoided. Every mistake is expensive. Every unforced error is painful.

Consider the last two hires you made.

- What was your state of mind when selecting the new hires? (Upgrading capabilities? Looking to fill the role quickly to alleviate stress on the system? Slow and steady until you found the perfect fit?)

- What questions did you ask to determine whether the person had the skills and capabilities needed to thrive in the role?

- What did you do to determine if the candidate's motivations aligned with what the role, and the organization, rewards?

- What data did you use to make your final selection decision?

- If you could bet your annual salary on whether the people you hired would thrive in their respective roles over the next twelve to twenty-four months, would you place that bet?

LOOK BEYOND TALENT

Wolfgang Amadeus Mozart was extremely gifted. In Geoff Colvin's book *Talent Is Overrated*[5], Colvin discusses Mozart's history and reveals that Mozart's father was a frustrated musician who never found success himself. To compensate for this failure, he immersed his children in music from day one, exerting more than a fair amount of pressure on them to succeed.

Mozart did amazing things as a child, but he did not wake up one day and just start composing music. His father significantly shaped the raw capacity that he brought to the table at a young age. The same can be said about people with truly exceptional capacity (talent or potential). Without the right input, they can end up performing at a less-than-exceptional level, regardless of innate talent or potential.

A more recent example that disrupts our traditional understanding of "talent" stems from an underlying belief among musicians that a small subset of people is born with "perfect pitch" and that this gift is the differentiator for their success in music. However, a recent study in Japan took a cluster of preschoolers and trained them to develop perfect pitch. About 95 percent of the children mastered this skill and went on to develop perfect pitch within twenty-four months. This debunks the myth that people are "just born with great talent" and reinforces that success is not determined by raw talent alone, but by a person's drive and commitment to learn and—what they do with the talent they have.

The belief many of us have that we are good at identifying people who bring specific talents to the table is unfounded. Moreover, as noted above, talent alone isn't the primary differentiator between good and great. To select the right people for any role, leaders need to understand the key behaviors (what needs to be done), competencies (how the work can most effectively be accomplished), and the motivating factors (what will move a person to action with zest). When we place people with the factors most associated with success in a given role in

---

5. Ken'ichi Miyazaki and Yoko Ogawa, "Learning Absolute Pitch by Children: A Cross-Sectional Study," Music Perception: An Interdisciplinary Journal 24, no. 1 (2006): 63–78, doi:10.1525/mp.2006.24.1.63.

that position, they are able to operate with the ease and energy needed to thrive.

When we assessed the job of an actuary, an ideal motivating factor we revealed using one of our SHIFT diagnostics was "collaborative." In the context of this job analysis, what we learned moved a person to action was operating behind the scenes, crunching numbers, analyzing data, and putting together presentations and reports—all to support the team's success. The people most successful in this role were not motivated by public credit for their work; in fact, they preferred staying out of the limelight.

If someone interviewing for this actuarial role shared, "I love working on a team. It makes me think creatively and I find it stimulating. I get energy from interaction with others," you would not be wise to put that person in this position. It doesn't matter how good their résumé is, how smart and competent they are, or how good they may be with numbers. Don't do it! The person is likely to either experience unproductive levels of stress, anxiety, and mental fatigue by consistently working in isolation, or they will become bored due to the lack of stimulation and direct engagement with colleagues. Over time, this mismatch of the person and the needs of the role will result in a negative impact on individual and team performance, and you will incur all the costs connected with replacing a team member.

It bears noting that the idea of capacity and job fit is not limited to new hires; it also applies to people who are already part of the organization. The assumption we see made is that a person performing well within a role in an organization should never leave that kind of role or industry. The basis for this belief is that accumulated knowledge is the key to or sole differentiator for success. In fact, while industry knowledge is relevant to performing well, it is just one component of success in a complex job. People can transition—sometimes with unbelievable speed—from one industry to another when they possess other factors related to high performance.

A friend of ours was a financial services representative for a few years right out of college. After a while, he decided he wanted to switch over to pharmaceutical sales, and he created a strategy to break into the industry. He networked to make meaningful connections, met people in the industry, and obtained referrals into opportunities that made sense for him. It took him two years, but he finally got an interview and was hired. At the time we were writing *THRIVE*, he was beginning his sixteenth year in pharmaceutical sales. Industry knowledge did not make him a good fit for that job; it was his drive and skill that made him successful.

BECOME AN EXEMPLARY PERFORMER

In addition to having the basic capacity to perform in a role, what facilitates someone becoming an exceptional performer? The literature about expertise refers to deliberate practice as the key differentiator. Perhaps the most widely recognized expert on the topic is Anders Ericsson, who states in his recent book, *Peak*:

> With deliberate practice, however, *the goal is not just to reach your potential but to build it*, to make things possible that were not possible before. This requires challenging homeostasis—getting out of your comfort zone—and forcing your brain or your body to adapt. But once you do this, *learning* is no longer just a way of fulfilling some genetic destiny; it *becomes a way of taking control of your destiny and shaping your potential in ways that you choose*. (emphasis added)[6]

We describe this as intentionality: the unwavering commitment to improve one's performance over time.

CASE IN ACTION

Kyle Schwarber played a significant role in the Chicago Cubs winning the 2016 World Series, even though he had been out due to an injury for

---

6. Anders Ericsson, *Peak* (Boston: Houghton Mifflin Harcourt, 2016), p. 48.

much of the season. His commitment to being ready and up to speed when he returned in time for the series was critical, and his play was a tipping point in the Cubs' victory.

When Schwarber first returned to practice, the doctor said he could only swing the bat sixty times a day. Most players would have gone into the batting cage, taken their sixty swings, showered, and gone home. However, he knew that it wasn't just the physical act of swinging that he had to bring up to speed again—world-class hitters need to see the rotation of the ball coming at them at a hundred miles an hour. Obeying the doctor's orders, Schwarber took his sixty swings, but he also watched additional pitches come across the plate from the pitching machine to improve his vision.

To give another example, Larry Bird took a thousand practice shots every day throughout his professional career. He didn't spend a mere few minutes on the basketball court. It took five or six hours per day to take that many shots—a clear example of deliberate practice.

It's easy to give these examples in athletics, but intentionality relates to all industries and fields. Greatness results from knowing what you want to accomplish, setting incremental goals for improvement, looking for opportunities to practice, getting feedback, and making progress.

Feedback is a component of optimal deliberate practice. Ideally, there is a coach or manager who can provide consistent, substantive feedback. When no coach is available, individuals need to establish an objective way to examine personal performance and make incremental changes to reach desired levels. Don't accept the adage "practice makes perfect." Practice makes permanent. Only perfect practice leads to perfect performance.

- How do I instill the practice of reflection in my organization?

- What is the evidence you see that individuals can and do objectively assess their performance and the make appropriate adjustments to improve results?

- What can I do to improve this skill and weave it into the fabric of my organization?

SKILLS AND KNOWLEDGE

Most leaders in major corporations believe that teaching people the individual components of their work will lead automatically to their putting the components together to perform the totality of the job. These components (skills or subskills) are called *competencies.* Using the word "competencies" to define these units of behavior is odd because saying someone is competent typically means that they can perform the entirety of their role at an appropriate level.

In Peak, Anders Ericsson provides the evidence that people master roles by practicing the components needed in their entirety. Success in the role does not occur if people are left to figure out how to put discrete competencies together in ways that apply to their specific role. Having subskills alone is insufficient to create sustained high levels of performance. Our experience shows that 85 percent of people who are taught individual competencies won't be able to perform the entirety of the work well. Accomplished performance is only achieved when they practice applying the skills needed in their role in an integrated fashion. There are many jobs for which a competency-by-competency approach is not only ineffective but unacceptable. The agencies responsible for regulating aviation would not let a pilot take flight who knows everything about aerodynamics, the plane's electronic systems, and the effects of the weather, but who never sat in a simulator and practiced with those factors integrated in actual scenarios. None of us would go to a medical doctor who has expertise in a certain area of knowledge but has never treated patients and apprenticed under the guidance of another skilled practitioner. People become good by doing the work under the guidance and coaching of highly proficient performers, not by simply learning about individual components of the work.

We strongly advocate for role-specific, on-demand learning, where people acquire the context-sensitive skills and knowledge needed to successfully produce the outcomes associated with their work, be it creating trusted customer relationships or diagnosing a system failure on the plant floor. We believe a significant part of role-specific development should be structured, on-the-job learning (SOJL). Employees can practice the work under the guidance of a competent peer or manager and improve over time, due to precise coaching and "perfect practice." This approach moves the focus away from memorization as the mechanism or measure by which competence is determined and toward evidence-based application of skills and knowledge. For example, we often see companies use training (online or classroom-based) as a major vehicle for the transfer of information from the trainer to the trainee, with the intention that the trainee will take what she learned and apply it in her work. In many cases, the issue with this approach is that the emphasis is on what the trainer does, as opposed to what the learner learns and can apply. Much of today's training focuses on presenting content rather than creating rich examples and providing practice opportunities. Presentation-heavy training assumes that when people are exposed to ideas, they will master the content. It is more effective to provide easy, real-time access to information, support, or subject-matter expertise as a performance accelerator while people are doing their actual work (or at least a simulation of the real conditions of doing their work). This active learning and application approach is a powerful mechanism for fostering higher levels of performance.

Many organizations are trending toward role-specific or context-specific development. A biopharmaceutical firm we worked with created replicas of doctors' offices in their training facility and staffed them with professional actors. Their sales training courses culminated with sales representatives going through a sales simulation after which they received feedback based on a video of their performance captured during the exercise. People should be trained and practice at the highest level that makes economic sense (using the stakes involved as a guide). For pilots, that means training in a multimillion-dollar flight simulator. As noted in the biopharmaceutical sales example, a full suite of doctors' offices staffed with professional actors was warranted. The approach for some businesses or roles might be much simpler. Regardless, the closer the practice is to the actual work, the greater the transfer.

Two of the most important decisions that need to be made for role-specific development are (1) whether or not information should be trained for recall, and (2) whether or not critical information should be stored outside of the individual performer in the form of performance support or job aids. Most trainers and instructional designers default to the assumption that all information should be stored in the heads of individuals and don't consider the alternatives.

Their formula for deciding what should be stored in people's heads and what should be available to them as an external reference, procedure, or job aid is tied to the complexity of the task, frequency of performance, and consequence of the error, among other factors. Most training, however, doesn't distinguish between what needs to be in memory and what can be provided by outside support. This lack of discernment leads trainers to provide all kinds of information that won't be rehearsed with any regularity, and therefore, it won't be recalled at the time of need. This approach wastes valuable time and money.

It is also important to consider the difference between delivering information and modifying behavior. Information can be stored and accessed at the time of need. Desired behavior must be modeled, coached, and reinforced. With these things in mind, many new-hire training programs would be much leaner in terms of information to be recalled and much richer in role-specific practice. A common—and flawed—approach is lumping people in twenty different roles into the same class to learn a competency they all need, such as communication skills. Remember that 85 percent of people who are taught a skill outside the context of the work itself will never apply the generic skill to their specific role. In a class of twenty people, that means seventeen won't use the skill or apply it well. This failure rate can be reversed when the skills are taught with role-specific practice and examples. Almost 100 percent of the people learning in that manner will transfer the new skill back to their own role.

MOTIVATION AND PREFERENCES

Why?

A simple and powerful word. When it comes to creating a thriving company, one in which individuals can truly be and accomplish their best, *why* plays a critical role.

As we've previously discussed, capacity, skills, and knowledge all have a part in the high-performance equation. Understanding why a person is drawn or compelled to do something is critically important. Leaders face complex challenges every day, and solutions are often hidden and messy. Navigating large, matrixed organizations can be confusing, frustrating, and just downright hard. Creating a barrier-free environment in which people can thrive every day is not for the faint of heart. To make this aspiration a reality, leaders must understand what truly drives each and every member of their team. Unfortunately, making this part of the conversation in organizations has not been a common practice. (Thanks to Simon Sinek, Adam Grant, and others, we have seen this begin to shift, but we've still got a long way to go.) The understanding and application of motivation and preferences applies to new candidates for employment as well as existing employees.

Traditional interviewing styles have conditioned potential candidates to strategize on how to "beat" an interview to get a job. Candidates layer their résumés with key buzzwords and phrases—they want to get past the algorithms that are designed to screen and eliminate ill-fitting candidates. Hiring managers tend to fixate on skills, knowledge, and lagging production indicators as their Rosetta stone of what creates successful employees. This myopic approach is pursued at the expense of understanding what really motivates the person they're speaking with and assessing. As a result of this oversight, the hiring process cannot include whether or not the person's motivators tightly align with what is most important to the company, the business unit, the team with whom this person will work every day, and her functional role. In the tight labor market in which most recruit for highly skilled talent, employers often spend too much time, too soon in interviews, trying to sell the candidate on why she should work at the company. Interviews tend to lack the depth, substance, and honesty required to make well-informed decisions by either party. This unfortunate game of "winning" the interview results in a losing scenario for the individual, the company, and the company's clients.

Effective selection requires that leaders get to the heart of this issue: has the candidate demonstrated a shared value and belief system that validates *why* this specific work matters to her? Without that connection, the ceiling on performance is lower and the performance less sustainable.

At SHIFT, part of our value system is caring. We are crystal clear on what caring looks like, and we illuminate this understanding with excellence indicators—what is happening and what gets said when a person operates in a caring way with clients and with his colleagues. We've identified the business outcomes that result from performing inspiring, results-obsessed work, delivered in a caring manner. We can say, for example, "As a result of us being the most caring consulting firm, clients view us as an extended part of their organization." We know that clients invite us into out-of-scope conversations for help and take a personal interest in what's happening in our world. We use the interview as a forum to explore the candidate's relevant thinking and behavior by asking questions like "Drawing on your experience as [pick one or two of their previous roles], give us the top two examples of how you've actively demonstrated care for your clients" and/or "Give us an example of providing care for a client who was going through a challenging time." It's fair to ask about a time when things didn't turn out as they'd planned or hoped...and what they did then.

Understanding a candidate's motivation and preferences—why they do what they do—provides a window into that person's soul. It helps to indicate whether and to what degree she will be resilient in challenging times or crumble under stress. It can suggest the likelihood of someone passionately running to the work every day or hitting the snooze button five times to ward off the dread of what lies ahead on a Monday morning. This alignment among an individual's *why*, the person's role, and the mission of the organization accelerates engagement and performance. More precise hiring necessitates that organizations also install specific processes before the actual hire. For example, consider recruiting posts. When sharing an opportunity on social media, or when working with a recruiter, the role vision must connect with the vision and values of the organization. It must bring the ethos of the firm to life, not just communicate a requirement of three to five years of relevant experience, with a certain volume of production.

One of the longest-standing and biggest areas of mistakes made by managers is making hiring decisions based principally on gut feelings. Let's be clear: we all have instincts, and until or unless they're validated through questioning, assessment, and skills demonstrations, those instincts are nothing more nor less than the bias we develop over time and through our specific experiences. We mentioned the bias of pharmaceutical companies hiring former cheerleaders for sales positions, an approach—like many—that is quickly revealed for the nonsense that it represents when organizations question preconceived notions early and often.

We noted the use of assessments above. When applying diagnostic tests such as the Myers-Briggs, Hogan Assessments, or TTI DNA profiles, it is important that hiring managers use the candidate's results as a guide to conduct better interviews. Failure to do so (a common occurrence) is mistake number one. The next mistake is making hiring decisions that contradict the diagnostic data. There can be times when going off script works out, but—even with acceptable levels of performance—damage may result from reinforcing or seeming to endorse undesired and undesirable behavior. "I went with my 'gut' and didn't follow the data, and look, the employee is amazing." In those cases, luck likely is in play. Remember, as in gambling, the house always wins. For better and more sustainable results, use data available.

Hiring a new employee is the beginning, rather than the end, of the process of creating and maintaining alignment. Ensuring that an individual finds meaning in her work is a critical aspect of one's leadership role. Doing so serves to inspire and foster even more discretionary effort and higher levels of performance. This responsibility isn't the sole domain of the leader; the employee can and should play an active role too. Inviting this partnership and actively facilitating it leads to the benefits of more engagement, higher performance, and deeper loyalty or sense of commitment, and helps to avoid unwanted surprises.

Think about a time when a valued employee left your firm. She cited that she had an opportunity that was too good to pass up, or that it provided avenues for growth she didn't have with you. Even more, think about an employee with great talent and potential whose possibilities fizzled as he failed to bring what was expected to life. We too commonly see leaders point the finger at the person leaving or falling short of what the leader imagined they would do, saying things like "She was not motivated" or "He didn't work hard enough" or "She just couldn't make it work here." There can be some truth in those statements, yet our experience tells us that the organizational system is what failed that employee most. Raising how effectively you recruit and hire greatly reduces the likelihood that their employment story ends because of lost motivation, lack of talent, or some other endemic shortcoming. More likely is that his motivation and preferences, among other things, were no longer aligned with his role or personal vision, he did not know how to course correct (possibly due to a lack of connection with his direct supervisor or mentor at the company), and so he chose to travel a path outside your company.

Staying tightly aligned with current employees is critical to creating and sustaining high levels of engagement and performance. Consider:

- Do you know what motivates your direct reports?
- What can you do to better understand the motivation and preferences of your direct reports?
- Do your direct reports know what motivates the people they lead?
- How can you more effectively ensure alignment between individual motivations and they work those people do?

WHAT MISTAKES DO POTENTIAL EMPLOYEES MAKE?

Regardless of whether unemployment rates are high or low, leaders want to hire new employees who will make positive contributions on a consistent basis. Hiring organizations target people who are already employed, or who are entering or reentering the job market from upper-level education programs.

To get an upper hand, interviewees try to outmaneuver one another. They think about packaging themselves by saying the "right thing," giving the answers that their potential boss wants to hear. While the great comedian Groucho Marx famously resigned from the Friars Club, writing that "I don't want to belong to any club that would have me as a member," most of us want to be chosen to be members of the teams we try out for through the interviewing process. This is true even when we'd prefer not to play for said team. As a result, candidates think more about what they think employers are looking for and say what they think the employer wants to hear. This is at the expense of talking about themselves honestly and leads to bad matches and unhappy, unproductive employment experiences.

Employers play into this tendency—one could argue even invite it—by asking questions like "What's your biggest flaw?" This question (noted as a useless one at least twenty-five years ago by Dr. Paul Green in his video series about better hiring, *More than a Gut Feeling*) often elicits this response: "I work too hard. I have a tough time unplugging from work." Seriously? This question-and-answer dynamic is a sad dance between interviewers not knowing or getting to the point of criteria that lead to success or failure in the jobs in their organizations, and candidates thinking and acting like students trying to say what the teacher wants them to in order to get an A instead of learning. This dual shortfall in truthfulness ends up in disappointment for everyone involved.

Even when they're asked inadequate questions, candidates can positively influence the process. Take the broad and dull inquiry of "What's your greatest flaw?" Candidates might ask in return, "I'm happy to share—context can be important—what are the main reasons you see people fail in this role or at this company?" More directly—and comfortably—they might say, "One person's flaw can be another's asset. I think my passion to develop diverse and inclusive cultures can sometimes slow down the near-term productivity that many companies value over all else." They might expand that further into an inquiry of their own, noting, "It's important that I work for an organization that values diversity and inclusion. I'd love to hear the company's stance on this topic and how you're bringing your ideas to life."

While these types of conversations are rare, you can see the potential for the rich dialogue that leads to insights that produce better decisions for all parties. This is the reason to push beyond the surface-level-talk tracks designed to allow employers and candidates blindly meet the goal of getting the job filled.

When employers passively or actively allow candidates to "win" the interview and be hired, the afterglow of filling the role and the honeymoon period of new employment will begin to wear off within the first six months. You can take that to the bank. The rose-colored glasses come off, and the employee sees what was there all along. Their internal (and sometimes external) narrative includes observations like "The way we do things around here is odd," "I don't like having to turn those reports in all the time," "Our customers are so demanding," "My manager doesn't listen to my ideas," "I didn't realize it was going to be this way," "I didn't think it was going to be this hard," and "There's so much ambiguity." These are just a few of the things we hear—all the time—when the selection process is more about checking the box than truly meeting the needs of the role.

Candidates need to approach job interviews with an actively discerning eye and prepare with proactive research and a commitment to find out if and how they'll truly be engaged working for an organization. They have, as resources, everything from online search to sites full of information about employers, like Glassdoor, Facebook, and LinkedIn. It's easy to find out about a company's culture—what they say it is and how those who work or have worked there say. Employers should use the selection process to provide realistic job previews. Candidates should demand them.

CAN PEOPLE AND COMPANIES STILL WIN WITHOUT TIGHT ALIGNMENT?

A person can still do a job even if their behaviors, competencies, and motivators don't align with what's ideal in a role. Someone may be good on the phone but uncomfortable talking to others in person or doing group presentations. It doesn't mean they can't do those things, but it does mean that they will likely experience a higher tax on their physical and mental energy than necessary. Remember, your aim is to create a barrier-free work environment, one in which people can do and be their best work every day, with little to no unnecessary stress or friction.

Consider a salesperson with a passion for serving existing customers. She gets energy from deepening relationships, takes pride in how much customers rely on her, and often highlights the things she knows about customers (e.g., how long customers have been connected with the organization and how much revenue she has generated as a byproduct of the strong customer relationships she had built). You decide to shift her focus to new-business generation. This role's primary aim is to attract new customers, handing them off to someone else for ongoing service. From your perspective, this is a great opportunity for her to earn more money. She doesn't seem as fired up as you thought she would be. She might be able to meet the new role's requirements, but that isn't really, or shouldn't be, the point. Leaders who facilitate stronger engagement and higher performance strive to create environments that encourage their people to do their best work every day. These are habitats in which people experience energy gain through their work, not energy depletion. This energy doesn't come solely—or even mainly—from money. A culture of high performance requires alignment between what the role requires and what drives the individual. Put the right people in the right roles in the right organizations and you get the best from and for everyone.

- Think about things you do every day that give you energy. What are they, and why do you get energy from them?

- Think about things you do every day that deplete your energy. What are they, and why do you lose energy because of them?

- What is one thing you can start doing to create more alignment between the roles in your organization and the people who fill those roles?

HOW/WHERE DO MOTIVATIONS AND PREFERENCES FIT WITHIN THE PERFORMANCE CYCLE?

To be most effectively self-directed and best mesh with our colleagues, we need to fine-tune our understanding of what drives us (self-awareness) and what drives others (social awareness).

Self-direction is illustrated by the former NFL player Michael Oher.[7] The real-life athlete portrayed in the movie The Blind Side (based on the book The Blind Side: Evolution of a Game), Oher wrote his autobiography because he felt the movie failed to accurately portray him as a person.

Oher grew up in the slums of Memphis. His mother would disappear for days at a time. At the age of eight or nine, Oher and his older brother essentially lived on their own. He was committed to hard work and improving his life before the family represented in The Blind Side took him under their wing.

7. Michael Oher, *I Beat the Odds: From Homeless, To The Blind Side, and Beyond* (New York: Gotham Books/Penguin, 2012).

After being drafted by the Baltimore Ravens, he showed up to the gym early every morning, and he stayed late on the practice field every evening. He understood that a better player could always come along and take his position, but he would never lose his spot by failing to put in his best effort every day of his life. He didn't set goals for the season; he set goals for the day. He was driven by the desire to improve his life, and he pushed himself to his limit to do just that.

When we seek to best align as teams and do so in ways we can keep up over time and not be run down by, we need to assess the chemistry between how we operate, how others do, and how those mix together. While working with a high-performing team in a sales organization, we discovered that a key relationship manager (RM) was driven largely by being *collaborative*. Specifically, this RM was driven by a sense of servant leadership: helping others win and moving the team forward, while working behind the scenes. Helping the team win was his recognition.

 Download at thrive.shiftthework.com/accelerators

Two of the RM's team members—people in roles dedicated to generating new business—were driven by collaboration's opposite number: *commanding*. They were motivated by status, recognition, and autonomy. Neither of these driving forces, commanding or collaboration, is good or bad. They are different. In certain circumstances, the nature of these differences can cause strain or even fracture.

In this case, the two commanding people operated as if every task or request required a high-urgency response. They moved at a fast pace and wanted to follow through with action items quickly. From their perspective, responsiveness was directly linked to their ability to win new deals. The new-sales-focused individuals often reached out to the RM for support with tasks related to new prospect and new client needs. The RM, with a driving force to support his colleagues, never said "no" to any of their requests.

When the RM described his working style and schedule to us, we knew it was not sustainable. He got up at six in the morning to respond to emails, and then took his children to school. He worked until six in the evening, and then took a break for dinner and family time.

He resumed working again until eleven at night. This was his Monday-through-Friday routine, and he often worked weekends. *Yikes!*

The RM was running himself into the ground. A couple of weeks after we spent time with his team, we learned he was in the hospital with a bleeding ulcer—a physical manifestation of his stress. This example does not mean that someone with a collaborative driving force can't succeed in an RM role, or in an RM role with colleagues who have a commanding driving force. This does illuminate, though, the importance of understanding why people do what they do. Going back to recruiting and hiring, it's essential to understand a person's *why* so they can be placed in the correct role and on the right team. It's not only critical to understand what drives people to do the things they do; in a team environment, it's essential for each team member to know what motivates the others, so situations like the one above can be avoided.

Fortunately, the story about this team of three had a happy ending. We held a recalibration session with them, discussing each of their driving forces and behaviors, and how they operate. Holding a mirror up to each of them and all of them allowed them to better align on their top priorities. They now have more productive ways to set boundaries, avoiding the weight of living in a world in which everything is a high priority. Each person now weighs in on the relative importance of tasks, and choices are made that ease the sense of burden and instead infuse the work with energy. It seems counterintuitive, but—by slowing down their frenetic pace—their output has increased.

HOW AND WHERE DO MOTIVATION AND PREFERENCES FIT WITHIN CAREER PLANNING?

In many organizations, employees receive promotions in recognition of consistently high performance. Too often, promotions move people into roles they're not prepared for, can't perform, and/or would prefer not to perform. This well-intentioned and wrong-headed approach to rewarding contribution in one role by placing someone in another role is particularly acute when it comes to moving high-performing individual contributors into roles that require contributing through others (e.g., supervisory or management positions). This default to promotion as a reward is dangerous to the health of the organization and its people, and it exists largely because leaders have not put other options in place to acknowledge high performance.

When leaders promote someone into a role in which the requirements and incentives do not align with the driving forces of the individual, the individual's performance will degrade as will the performance of those around them. Despite feeling frustrated, unfulfilled, anxious, and more, the promoted employee is likely to stay with the firm. They probably are more highly compensated and certainly are expected to facilitate others' success. Promotions that ignore alignment, not to mention preparation, are a net negative and should be avoided. Creating opportunities for growth and mobility, in addition to vertical advancement, are essential if an organization is to nurture a broad range of talented people and get the best from them in ways that result in the whole being greater than the sum of its parts.

Employee motivators should be considered in supporting transitions overall—from promotion to role change to offboarding. Such consideration is all too rare. Maintaining honest dialogues that include job holders' personal preferences and motivators enables the employer and employee to uncover and pursue intentional work transitions, including to a different role and even to a different organization.

CASE IN ACTION

We had a team member who was a phenomenal cultural fit at SHIFT. In her role as a recruiter, she was a fantastic team player and brought our organizational values to life in how she operated with our clients, candidates, and colleagues; she was passionate and always had new ideas. She referred potential new employees to us and was an energizing force with our client accounts. Clients loved her, but she had poor performance in delivering recruiting results.

The goal at SHIFT for someone in her role is to place two or three people per month, and this team member had gone six months without making a placement. This aligned with neither our performance expectations nor her earning needs. She wasn't winning, and she knew it. Not wanting her to toil through the process, we worked with her by giving her extra training and listening to her interviews and calls. After a while, she told us that, even though she wholeheartedly believed in our mission, recruiting for multiple clients just wasn't part of her why, and she wanted to look for a situation that would allow her to perform at her best.

The key point of this example is that she got in front of the conversation. She put together a transition plan for the next thirty days to help us find a replacement for her, and she continued working on accounts and client relationships. She left the organization in absolutely the right way.

It's rare to see an employee with the courage to have that conversation with her boss, but it doesn't have to be! In that thirty-day transition period, this team member placed four people. She left on good terms, which doesn't happen often in many companies. Her exit did not prompt any criticism of her, which sent a positive message to the people that remained in the organization. When an employee exits a company, those who remain employed watch and listen for how the organization talks about and treats people who have left. If they are treated with dignity and respect, employees will be more open and willing to have a proactive conversation with their manager when in a similar situation.

IN SUMMARY

For an organization and its employees to thrive, there must be alignment of the three individual influences: capacity and job fit, skills and knowledge, and motivation and preferences. Competencies are not the only factors that shape success, and the employee's level of talent does not guarantee performance excellence. The three individual influences reflect the totality of an individual, and none outweighs the others—they must all fit together in a harmonic mosaic.

- In your organization, where do you see tight alignment across the three individual influences?

- In your organization, where do you see lack of alignment across the three individual influences?

- In the areas of misalignment, what, specifically, will you do to improve this?

ANALYZE "STAR" EMPLOYEES

Understanding precedes action.

—RICHARD SAUL WURMAN, FOUNDER OF TED

⚡ CHAPTER 4 ACCELERATORS

While studying high-performing general managers for one of our clients, we saw a large variance in performance across more than eight regions and eighty markets. During our analysis, we did see that a small number of the markets produced a significant portion of the company's revenue. Looking deeper into the data, we saw that even fewer markets outpaced all others on a consistent basis. Levels of performance against company goals or market competitors were not attributed to specific regions, market size, tenure of the general manager, or even the performance of the local economy. We were inspired to learn the factors contributing to the results of the highest-performing markets so we could scale what we learned across the rest of the organization.

During our study, we uncovered some things that the best general managers did that were invisible to the rest of the organization. These included:

- *Having a consistent approach to building a market strategy plan*
- *Having specific processes, practices, and principles for building a winning culture*

From the high-performing general managers' perspective, producing these plans and a winning culture were critical factors in their ability to consistently beat the competition and exceed company goals. At the time of our analysis, nowhere in the company onboarding or training for general managers were these things taught.

THE REALITIES OF HIGH PERFORMANCE

There are false assumptions about high performance and high-performers that nevertheless are predominant in our businesses and in our culture. One such assumption is that high performance is singularly attributable to raw talent or raw capacity. This leads to the false belief that the only way to obtain top performers is to hire exceptional talent.

Our more than sixty years of experience in decoding exemplary performance enables us to codify transferable components of excellence and success that can be taught to and learned by an entire role population. The clarity of performance criteria positively impacts businesses through more accurate and precise hiring, reduced time to full competency, more efficient business processes, targeted coaching, meaningful performance management, and reduced regrettable attrition.

Companies go out of their way to retain high performers, while doing nothing to replicate their performance. This incongruity stems from our misdirected belief in the source of high performance, which causes us to ignore the size or impact of performance gaps. Their size and impact are significant and, at times, even staggering. The differences in performance we observe are a given, we tell ourselves; our team is operating along a normal distribution curve. Unsubstantiated belief leads us to false assumptions and results in our failing to seek to understand—much less leverage—exceptional contributors. If we did, we would be able to elevate the overall performance of the team.

The gap between good and great increases with the complexity of work. Someone doing repetitive work on an assembly line doesn't need a high level of experience, and performance is consistent among most employees. However, if we look at skilled tradespeople who maintain equipment on the line, the work is more complex, performance variance increases among the workers, and the risk to the business increases.

In our work with skilled tradespeople, we typically find a few qualified individuals who know how to repair equipment faster and return the line to full operation more quickly than most of their peers. When a system failure occurs, it's a good bet the organization will reach out to one or more of these exceptional people—even if they are off shift. They call in one of these highly qualified individuals because restoring the line to full production is of high value. The people they tap are their so-called go-to people. This is considered to be a good thing but comes with an all-too-often overlooked risk: the members of this select group of highly proficient people whom we call on, over and over, are more likely to experience burnout, low morale, and disengagement—the exact opposite of what organizations want for their most valued and valuable people.

CASE IN ACTION

Consider Karen, an exceptional team member. She receives a phone call from the plant because a manufacturing line is down. She gets out of bed to come in, and she's able to get the line up and running faster than anyone else who was already on shift. How could this process be improved so Karen doesn't have to get out of bed, and someone on-site can resolve the problem?

There are components of high performance that are transferable, and documenting Karen's procedure for diagnosing and fixing the line is a possible solution. If the organization had captured Karen's expertise and that information was made available to everyone, they would know how to restore the line more quickly. Someone on-site could take care of the issue, and it wouldn't be necessary to call Karen back to the plant. Imagine what you would do if Karen were getting ready to retire. That would exacerbate the importance of building a more robust and scalable approach to knowledge capture, sharing, and management.

THE IMPORTANCE OF CASE-BASED ANALYSIS

When studying high performance, we analyze right to left—from strategy, to accomplishment, to behaviors, to influences. We start our analysis by setting up a project-alignment meeting with the key stakeholders together in one room. The process begins with us hearing from with the leaders who set goals, design strategies, and establish expectations for the project. They understand the accomplishments or results needed by the roles we're analyzing (directly and for the overall success of the organization). We then hold an alignment session with the full group to uncover differing views of what is most important. This difference or disagreement about how success is defined and measured in certain roles can occur even at the highest levels of an organization. Further analysis is pointless unless or until leaders are aligned.

FIGURE 4.1

TYPICAL APPROACH TO PERFORMANCE

| PEOPLE ARE EQUIPPED | TO PERFORM TASKS | THAT PRODUCE OUTCOMES | THAT ACHIEVE GOALS |

SHIFT'S APPROACH TO PERFORMANCE

| DETERMINE INFLUENCES | ANALYZE TASKS | DETERMINE OUTPUTS OF VALUE | ★ DEFINE SUCCESS |

We work with the people who are concerned with and knowledgeable about specific roles. Rather than working with the CEO of a manufacturing company, we'd likely connect with the plant manager and leaders in areas like engineering and quality control. In a sales organization, we might choose the chief revenue officer as our primary point person.

Once we understand the critical results or accomplishments needed from the role, we can work with senior leaders to identify the high performers—those employees who consistently produce the desired results at a high level. If we started by asking, "Who are your best performers?" our results would be arbitrary. Leaders might tell us to talk to a certain person because they have been there for a long time. They may have us meet with an average performer so their company won't lose the time and productivity of the high performer. By conducting our analysis from right to left (starting with the outcomes and working back to the people who produce them), we enable leaders to select high performers based on the metrics that matter. We now can use interviews and observations of exemplary employees to identify key performance indicators (or excellence indicators), key actions, essential resources, and other critical variables required for superior results.

Case-based analysis allows you to be "lean" in terms of what good performers need to change in order to produce results more closely aligned with the highest performers. Without tying the analysis to an actual case, the information will be at too high a level to be helpful. Simply asking a high performer to tell you the things they do to produce key results risks having the employee unintentionally skipping over essential items and leaving out the needed detail. A more specific inquiry yields a more specific reply, like (in the case of sales) "Show me an example of a recent proof of concept and walk me through the process. I want to know what triggered the decision to create it. Take me all the way to the analysis."

All of this allows us to create a map of the required work to yield the intended accomplishments. With that guide in hand, you are able to assess each of the six influences in the Exemplary Performance System (EPS) and determine what needs to be done to both eliminate barriers and raise the level of performance throughout the organization.

A number of years ago, we were asked to evaluate the training provided by a paint booth vendor for an automobile assembly plant. In addition to the booth, the equipment vendor also provided training for the operators on the assembly line. Once the design phase of the project was complete, the design engineers were assigned to develop the training.

When we reviewed the training, we discovered a four-hour module about the viscosity of paints. Different color paints have slightly different thicknesses, and this information was extremely relevant to the engineers—they had to design the nozzles to evenly coat the vehicles, and knowing the viscosity was essential for their role. However, for the paint booth operators, the desired outcome was a vehicle with a high-quality finish. All they needed to know was how to adjust the controls to apply different colors properly. Knowing the thickness of red versus black didn't have an impact on the painters' outcome—they just needed to apply the paint correctly, so the four-hour training module was unnecessary for the painters' role.

Most organizations will refer to subject-matter experts (SMEs) as the source of information, insights, and best practices for aligning the six influences of the EPS versus using exemplary performers. Occasionally, SMEs and high performers are the same people, but often, they are not. SMEs know why things work the way they do, but they may not be able to produce the desired outcomes themselves. In contrast, high performers consistently produce excellent results, but may not be fully aware of the underlying "science" of the system or process.

ROLE EXCELLENCE PROFILES

We use a tool at SHIFT called the Role Excellence Profile (REP). The REP is a powerful, outcomes-based approach designed to shift the performance in the majority of your workforce to higher levels of contribution that are significantly more profitable. The Role Excellence approach focuses on identifying what makes your top performers tick and what they actually do to be so effective. These insights are then laid out in a performance map that is used to guide others to replicate those behaviors. Through interview, observation, and case-based analysis, exemplary performers reveal what is needed to accelerate the performance of the entire organization.

Typically, the vast majority of business results are produced by a small percentage of the individuals in a given role. The REP enables you to unlock the potential of the rest of your workforce by:

- Codifying the primary accomplishments and outcomes produced by top performers in their role
- Capturing explicit indicators of success
- Identifying top performers' key actions
- Highlighting accelerators of and barriers to higher levels of performance

Having homed in on the factors necessary for achieving excellence in specific roles and enabling the systems to focus on and drive the right behaviors, you'll benefit from:

- More consistent and predictable performance
- Shorter time to competence
- Streamlined training, saving time and money
- More time spent creating value for customers and your company
- Increased revenue and profits

REPs should be performed only for roles that produce results that are critical to the success of the organization: results that support the strategy of the enterprise. The goal is not for people to be busier; rather, we want them to be more successful.

The average role is responsible for producing four to six primary accomplishments. Once we understand the must-have accomplishments for a critical role, we use them to select the individuals or, sometimes, the teams that consistently produce superior outcomes. We perform case-based analyses, typically in the natural work setting(s) for the role. The analyses, whenever possible, include real-time observation. Following the analyses, we map the accomplishments back to the behaviors, and then determine what an employee (novice through seasoned veteran) needs to know in order to replicate the appropriate behaviors and produce the same valuable results.

High performers typically find ways to succeed no matter the state of the overall work system. Lack of feedback or easy access to resources won't slow them down. They set up their own methods of performance measurement and find ways to get what they need to do the job. If they are overloaded or stretched too thin, they come up with an algorithm for prioritization in order to produce important results in a timely fashion. They know which requests to ignore, and which meetings to skip. We capture their mental models through in-depth observations. All of this goes into improving and more effectively aligning all six EPS influences. The exemplar's insight and ability to optimize their own performance while navigating a broken system provides data that reduces or eliminates a wide range of work barriers.

The bulk of the performance variance in a role is due to higher performers' ability to successfully navigate complex and often suboptimal systems while still producing great results. The REP reveals the excellence indicators used by high performers, which tend to be more sophisticated than the indicators or metrics used by their organization. High performers typically have identified effective leading or predictive indicators of success, such as quality and strength of relationships. Most organizational metrics or key performance indicators are limited to the results themselves, like revenue or market share growth. Those are lagging indicators.

High performers understand measuring progress against leading indicators is a critical part of their overall success. High-performing salespeople don't track next quarter's quota; they track leading indicators that show them if they're going to meet or exceed that quota—often multiple quarters into the future. Their indicators might include a sales pipeline, but they also may include something subtle and unique to the high performer—something they've never thought to share with anybody else. This individual metric seems so obvious and comes so naturally to them that they assume everyone else is doing things the same way.

Even in an organization where the six arrows are not fully aligned, the REP still can be impactful, as it creates clarity for how to succeed in their role. They are, nonetheless, working against broader forces within the organization—seeking to thrive despite the organizational influences, not because of them.

In highly aligned organizations, where all employees are clear on the vision, values, goals, and strategies, the REP is an amazing tool. It a blueprint of the simplest version of what high performance looks like for a given role or team.

The REP documents the following key aspects of the role:

Accomplishment Details	Primary accomplishment Importance Difficulty Indicators of success Interactions Tools/resources
Influences	Accelerators Barriers
Tasks	Key tasks Frequency (of the key tasks)

⚡ Download at thrive.shiftthework.com/accelerators

Creation of the REP does more than document key attributes of top performers; it contains the details needed to design a well-targeted learning path, both to onboard new performers and to better equip average-performing incumbents. This makes the REP a powerful design point for a role-based curriculum (or role-base curricula), the recommendations for which we articulate in a focused curriculum map.

⚡ Download at thrive.shiftthework.com/accelerators

Our REP methodology is the result of over twenty-five years of refining approaches to intentionally developing and supporting higher levels of performance. First practiced by Thomas Gilbert, one of the early thought leaders in the field of human performance, our approach shifts the process from listing what people know and do to focusing on what they produce that adds value to the business.

We use these outcomes to illuminate the cognitive expertise, mental models, and tasks required to produce these critical results. This reorientation is what makes our approach such a game changer. By starting with what's most important to the company, we are able to focus any essential individual roles within the business on exactly what they need to contribute to the company's overall ability to deliver as intended.

The power of the REP approach is illustrated in figure 4.2. The horizontal axis represents the level of performance based on producing valued outcomes for the business. The level of performance plotted here is not based on credentials, potential, talent, training, years of experience, or competencies. It is based on produced outcomes that yield valued business results. It spans the range from minimum to average to top performers.

The vertical axis represents the percentage of workforce operating at the various levels of performance. As in most distributions, the majority of performers are at the center of the distribution, as represented by the vertical line labeled "average."

There are some performers who are operating at less-than-average performance. Typically, there is a minimally acceptable level of performance, below which the performer/job match becomes questionable. At the other end of the spectrum, however, there are the top performers who consistently produce exceptional business results.

There is considerable value to be accessed by studying how top performers consistently outperform others. Companies can realize substantially improved business and financial results by leveraging this knowledge to develop interventions that shift the levels of performance of the "average" closer to that of the "top."

FIGURE 4.2

THE PERFORMANCE CURVE

The shaded area illustrates this shift in the performance curve, which creates a new standard. The opportunity cost in play can be greater than 50 percent when comparing average to top performers...and in moving average performers toward top performance.

WHEN SHOULD A COMPANY USE THE REP?

Companies should use the REP every time excellent performance of a role or group of roles is critical to the success of a business unit and/or the broader organization. Though everyone's contributions matter, not all roles make a critical difference. The REP informs success criteria throughout the employee life cycle. It is the design inspiration for a high-impact learning curriculum, and its components are relevant in recruitment, hiring, coaching, performance optimization, and career mobility. Knowing what top performers do to produce outcomes of value allows us to take a lean approach to learning and performance (see figure 4.3). Individuals focus on learning only the critical subject matter that helps them perform in ways that create maximum performance acceleration and impact in their role. Leaders can facilitate this process by developing a curriculum map (see Appendix B for a sample) for which content is developed to train average performers and new employees in the role.

We know that an REP may be needed when a role:

- Is customer-facing
- Has high performance variability among role incumbents
- Significantly impacts the business results
- Exposes the organization to a high degree of risk
- Is critical to the successful rollout of a new business strategy or transformation
- Has high turnover resulting in significant impact to customers and/or onboarding costs

Download at thrive.shiftthework.com/accelerators

Once our analysis reveals the primary accomplishments of top performers, we create the curriculum map and employee journey map. The required elements of the programs and the preliminary learning activities required are identified using the primary accomplishments. Closely tying the curriculum to the accomplishments documented in the REP and cross-referencing the accomplishments to curriculum units ensures a focused, effective learning experience for those in the role. The highly focused curriculum map provides the foundation for the more-detailed content design and development work that follows.

FIGURE 4.3

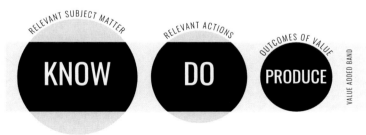

Source: Exemplary Performance®

ROLE-BASED CURRICULUM MAP

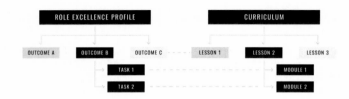

Our curriculum design principles include:

- Begin with a focus on performance and business outcomes
- Identify individual behaviors and tasks that yield outputs necessary for desired business outcomes and the success criteria for each of those outcomes
- Eliminate extraneous lessons, content, and interventions that can distract performers from what matters most
- Build performance-based programs and evaluation plans

In addition to driving revenue through performance, benefits of the REP to the business include:

- Selection criteria for new performers
- Expectation-setting, measurement, and feedback processes
- Goal setting and performance inventory
- Input to individual development plans
- Framework for precise coaching

The outcomes uncovered during the REP process form the backbone of an integrated performance system. This integrated performance system enables both individuals and businesses to perform to their fullest potential. Figure 4.5 depicts the relationship of the REP and its accomplishments to the performance system. Please note that the more you can deploy this process and use online tools and resources, the easier it will be to accelerate learning and performance across any role population.

FIGURE 4.5

INTEGRATED PERFORMANCE SYSTEM

ROLE EXCELLENCE PROFILE

CAREER DEVELOPMENT PATH

JOB POSTING

ROLE-BASED CURRICULUM

PERFORMANCE ASSESSMENT

COACHING GUIDE

PERFORMER

COACH

Download at thrive.shiftthework.com/accelerators

IN SUMMARY

The REP is one of the most powerful tools and processes you can leverage to shift performance in your organization. Creating clarity around what excellent performance looks like and using that new standard as the design point for recruiting, hiring, onboarding, training, coaching, performance management, and career mobility can have a significant impact on your organization's top- and bottom-line business results. Now that we've outlined how you can use the REP, we'll next talk about how you can accelerate the change associated with elevating individual and organizational performance.

- Which roles are the most critical to your organization's success?

- Consider a top performer in each of these roles. What makes them better than the rest?

- Across the population of individuals in each of those roles, how large is the performance variance?

- What is the cost of that performance gap to your company?

- How are you actively working to create the same levels of performance across all people in these critical roles?

OH, THE PLACES YOU'LL GO!

You're off to great places!

Today is your day!

Your mountain is waiting, so...Get on
your way!

—DR. SEUSS

Acceleration.

Leaders often believe they know what it takes to perform a role at a high level because they used to hold that specific role. Maybe they do "ride-alongs" with their salespeople or frequently interact with people in the assembly plant or contact center. However, customer demands and the nature of work changes so rapidly today that when an individual has not performed a particular role for a period of six months or more, that manager loses perspective on what it takes to thrive in that role. You read that right—six months is all it takes to lose perspective. That is how fast technology, competition, customer buying preferences, and workflow changes today, and it's only getting faster. Simply put, leaders and managers often lack the context of what it takes to consistently perform at high levels in the roles they lead and manage.

Earlier, we shared that part of the REP creation process includes studying current high performers performing their work. Doing a field ride or shadowing a high performer does not equate to rigorous study—really understanding what someone does, along with how and why he does it. To replicate accelerated business results that align with organizational goals, you need to understand how high performers think. They have a different mental model and have developed cognitive expertise that is invisible to most others in the organization, especially leaders. Viewing a high performer's mind as a flow chart would reveal that they go through a different process when doing their work, especially when faced with organizational barriers. They move quickly to get through, around, over, or past those barriers. They think in ways that differ from others within the organization—the average performers.

When we see a high performer do something that facilitates advanced levels of performance, we ask that individual if everyone else in their role does the same thing, the same way. Almost always, the individual does not know for sure. For a high performer, it's intuitive to work a process in a certain way, so they assume everyone else is on the same page. Because organizations often lack insight into the current best practices of high performers, and often don't share known best practices effectively, performance deceleration is unintentionally woven into the fabric of their company. When we discover a performance facilitator, the goal is to help organizations understand what it is and how to make it a part of the overall system.

Installing the EPS in your organization is all about accelerating business results by creating clarity, alignment, and a barrier-free work environment. The REP is a foundational tool and process in this system, but not enough to provide maximum acceleration.

Think about your favorite meal at your favorite restaurant. Envision the smell, the taste, the perfect ambiance, and the best beverage pairing that fully brings out the robust flavors of the food. Now, think about the preparation of that meal, all the way back to the recipe. The recipe alone does not bring that meal or that dining experience to life. It takes deliberate practice, repetition, a deep understanding of how the ingredients complement each other, and an appreciation for the variety of spices, the beverages, and how each plays a role in delighting the palate. The same holds true for producing a new standard of performance in a role. The REP is your recipe. Accelerating change results from bringing that recipe to life in all of the areas that influence performance. For example, the REP can inform how the recruitment arm of an organization creates job postings and social media posts that more accurately reflect what is required to thrive in the role. It can also help managers more precisely coach an individual to perform critical tasks consistently and with higher levels of proficiency. These examples specifically tie to the Expectations and Feedback arrow.

When it comes to change, we often see leaders take action based on flawed assumptions and a lack of understanding of how to effect positive change. For example, leaders have a tendency to think that because they said or wrote something once, those on the receiving end of the message fully understand and have internalized the full context of what the sender intended. Sending an email to a team, department, business unit, or the entire organization to share that the company has a new strategy, service, product, or process is not change management. Simply saying, "Do things this way from now on" just doesn't work (try it with your children). The process of change is much more complex, and it isn't just about changing the way people behave.

Behavioral change is necessary in any transformation, but to effectively engage others, and have them take ownership of leading, managing, and landing the desired change, leaders first need to affect the way that people at all organizational levels think about the change:

what it is, why the change is important, why it matters to the individual, and how the individual's efforts connect to the bigger picture, all while creating an environment where every person can take ownership of what is changing (and what isn't).

The REP can be used to bring about positive, sustainable change that supports high performance. When all six arrows of the EPS are not appropriately aligned, however, people inevitably revert to old ways of thinking. That's why over 70 percent of change and transformation efforts fail to deliver the intended business results. Consider what happens when a company launches a new sales training program. An employee attends a training course, and she returns motivated and inspired. She wants to implement the new things she learned, but after a while she reverts to her old ways. Why? Because she has not changed the way she thinks about performance and has neither created nor committed to a personal case for change. The same thing happens when a new technology or business system gets introduced. In many cases, the end user of the system, who was far removed from the goals, strategy, and design thinking with the new system, doesn't understand how or why her work has changed, so she creates personal work processes outside of the new system so she can operate in the same or similar fashion to how she operated previously. This totally undermines the intent and effectiveness of the organizational transformation. Thinking back to the EPS, the influences of Motivation and Preferences, Expectations and Feedback, and Rewards, Recognition, and Consequences have not been appropriately addressed. With this lack of alignment, leaders should expect inconsistent results and an employee whose fundamental belief structure hasn't changed ("Training doesn't work"; "I won't ever be great at sales"; "I don't know why they designed the system this way. It doesn't work for me").

Sustainable change is nonnegotiable when it comes to pursuing high performance. As a leader, you have to address individual and organizational mindsets and belief structures and have clear, aligned definitions of success. There is a sustained, long-term change process that goes with this rewiring, and that's why we start with alignment at the executive level. To redefine the meaning of success, leaders need to align organizational goals, and those changes must permeate the entire organization.

AMPLIFY AND ACCELERATE IMPACT AND RESULTS

If you want to go fast, go alone.
If you want to go far, go together.

—AFRICAN PROVERB

CHAPTER 5 ACCELERATORS

TIGER TEAMS

BALANCED SCORECARD

A CHRO of a global organization asked our team to help her elevate individual and team performance for her direct reports. During our intake conversation with our client, we learned that her team members were equipped with deep domain expertise, but struggling areas including self-awareness, team effectiveness, and operating as a strategic unit that could advance critical business priorities. We also learned that members of the team had a difficult time being completely honest with her, especially during moments of disagreement and conflict. This group consistently invested in training and development, applying a variety of tools, processes, and methodologies to improve engagement and performance, and yet they struggled to actualize their potential. One of the biggest issues they experienced was not being able to make decisions, take aligned and purposeful action to advance strategic plans, and deliver timely impact to drive business outcomes. Instead, they repeatedly revisited the same issues, even after decisions had been made, which resulted in disengagement, distrust, and disconnection.

Early in our time working with the group, what we discovered was that while they spoke often and discussed issues of strategic importance, their time together lacked the depth and substance required to make the meaningful progress expected of a team at this level in an organization. For example, we saw:

- Members of the team who monopolized conversations but did not advance progress through strategic or critical thinking

- Momentum and engagement stall because people refused to rein in discussions that got off track

- People withdraw from discussions, withholding their points of view and then criticizing the lack of progress and productivity of the sessions during breaks

During our first three months of working together, we pushed their team to productive levels of discomfort through active inquiry, questioning some of the things they felt must be true about organizational structure, the role of HR as business leaders, their service delivery model, and what was really required to be an effective member of this senior HR leadership team. After completing one segment of our work, the CHRO commented that through our approach and work with the team, we had made more progress with them in the first few months than they had in the previous eighteen months.

Trust is one of the greatest accelerators of organizational performance, and lack of trust is one of the greatest decelerators.

Inherently, people know this, yet many leaders fail to build this critical element into the fabric of the organization successfully. We have heard leaders say that they don't have time for the "soft stuff" and that "employees aren't customers." Talk about a lack of enlightenment and awareness. If you don't believe that trust is one of the most critical components in building a high-performance culture, we need to chat—NOW!

Easy ways to amplify trust in your organization include:

- Conducting employee engagement studies and sharing the results.
- Including frontline employees in developing solutions to challenges raised in engagement studies.
- Having regular one-on-ones with direct reports and conducting skip-level one-on-ones with employees who do not directly report to you. Ask questions and listen.
- Sending handwritten thank-you notes to employees, recognizing them for their contributions. Be specific, so they know exactly what you appreciate.
- Putting open-book management into practice.
- Producing a weekly state-of-the-union video message and sharing it with the company (or your department). Let people know what is on your mind, what is important to you, and where you need their help.
- Having zero tolerance for employees whose behavior does not align with the company vision and values.

When it comes to shifting performance, leaders must establish trust and gain buy-in to the organization's strategies. This alignment starts with the most senior leaders in the organization (which, oftentimes, is where we see alignment lacking the most). Remember the 25 Reasons Why exercise you did earlier? You can do this with your leadership team as well, having them list why this organizational transformation is a nonnegotiable for each of them, personally. Do the work individually and as a group. Just like in Remember the Titans, this is your leadership team's off-season workout. They must find common ground and deep-rooted connection, and form massive team commitment.

Here are two accelerators to increase the likelihood of buy-in to your transformation:

STEP ONE

Create a vision (for the organization and for any strategy) that conveys where you are going and why it matters. More than words on paper, the vision provides guidance as to what is most important and becomes a unifying mechanism across the company. Create and refine organizational values and the corresponding organizational behaviors that serve as guardrails for how individuals make decisions and operate day to day.

STEP TWO

Take the strategic planning process outside the ivory tower. Senior leadership is paid to make critical decisions, and they do need to set the course for an organization. That said, leaders also need to bring diverse thinking into this process. The days of three people designing the company strategy in isolation and then dictating to everyone else what they must do are long gone—that approach is outdated and ineffective. Today's approach must be inclusive, garnering input from within the organization. Whether through committees, focus groups, action learning projects, surveys, or a blend of these, people besides the most senior leaders must be included in the process. Leaders also need to leverage technology, creating space for online, face-to-face interactions so they can garner input from across the globe. This gets maximum traction in driving the strategy to successful execution.

GET THERE TOGETHER

Frontline employees must be involved in business transformation efforts, not only because they have the most intimate knowledge of the actual work that needs to be done, but also because involving them in the process increases their trust in leadership—it makes them advocates for the strategic changes at hand. People feel a sense of ownership when they have a voice, and that's what we're after. Ownership allows employees to actively participate in change, so they feel like things are happening *for* them, not to them.

To effectively engage people in the formulation and execution of a strategy, you must make it real to them. Once leaders draft overarching goals and strategies, engage employees in refining those strategies and developing the core tactics of executing them. One way to do this is through a process called **tiger teams**. Link the *big* goals to every business unit, department, team, and individual by forming small, cross-functional teams of employees. Provide executive sponsorship and advice to the groups so they have support, and give them the autonomy to build specific detail for the strategies and supporting tactics to achieve company goals.

 Download at thrive.shiftthework.com/accelerators

As an example, if one of the main goals for a firm is to grow the business through a customer intimacy strategy, a tiger team can build the pathways to achieve this goal. They might suggest doing some voice-of-the-customer work to ensure the company really understands customer needs and points of pain. The group might suggest deploying or enhancing real-time customer feedback mechanisms to increase flexibility and responsiveness. The power of having a cross-functional group drive these decisions includes:

- Direct involvement increases ownership and accelerates change management
- Tiger teams provide practical stretch assignments for employees, developing skills and capabilities needed to grow

- Involvement in tiger teams fosters pride in employees, and they become advocates for higher levels of engagement and performance
- Frontline employees are closer to the customers than executives, so their perspective is often more aligned to the actual customer experience than what leaders think

- What is an initiative or strategy you recently deployed that a tiger team could have made more effective?
- What is an important goal for which you can use a tiger team?

KEEP A MORE BALANCED SCORECARD

If you are an executive, you most likely have a scorecard that includes financial, operational, and service-oriented factors. Ideally, you have a balance of the areas that are measured and they align with organizational strategies, as opposed to just lagging revenue and profit targets. While understanding, owning, and driving lagging indicators is extremely important, when they become the sole focus, we can all but guarantee the organization will underachieve. Consider the impact to sustainable success if you measure throughput, revenue, and profit, without considering employee engagement, internal employee growth and promotions, succession planning, safety, quality defects, or customer sentiments.

Consider the related areas of succession planning and career development. If it's important to create a future generation of leaders and continue to develop high performers within the organization, there can't be a transactional churning of people. If high performance is truly a priority, you must focus on how you develop future leaders. Take three minutes to answer these four questions:

- Who is *your* successor?

- Who is that person's successor?

- Who does the documented company succession plan say are the next level of leaders behind the senior executives?

- What is the formal development plan to ensure those next-level leaders are ready to step into executive roles?

You can use questions like these to consider how to place leader development on dashboards and key performance criteria. If a company has a nationwide presence and thousands of employees, it probably means there are tons of opportunities that need to be made visible throughout the organization.

Employees need to know what opportunities are available, what to expect from the company in terms of succession planning, and how to access mentorship for growth. High performers also deserve an inside track or advantage over someone who sends in a cold résumé from outside the company. The organization should shine a spotlight on amazing talent and allow current employees to throw their hat in the ring for new positions. Unfortunately, we've seen organizations thwart engagement by doing the following:

- Hiring from the outside without giving current employees an opportunity to interview for new opportunities

- Offering disproportionate compensation packages to new employees in comparison to existing employees

- Interviewing current employees, giving roles to outside candidates, and not informing the current employees the key areas of needed development to strengthen prospects of future candidacy

A more balanced scorecard creates a healthy blend of people and culture, the elements that drive profitability, and key operations. With balanced metrics, you're much more likely to get the business results you desire. Imagine the diverse thinking and extra discretionary effort that is possible through a consistent effort to develop next-level leaders. This approach creates clarity, alignment, focus, and allows all departments and employees to see how their effort connects to the bigger picture. Identifying critical metrics or key performance indicators and weaving those metrics throughout the entire organization makes explicit to employees what they are accountable for and how they will be measured. It also allows them to see where their department or division stands. For example, you could use colors and a reporting status. Are the indicators green, yellow, or red? If they are green, individuals can keep doing what they're doing. However, if they're yellow or red, leaders can try to understand why their team isn't seeing the expected results and take the appropriate measures to correct the issues.

 Download at thrive.shiftthework.com/accelerators

Linking the EPS to this scorecard approach allows leaders to take an integrative approach that goes beyond simply telling people the metrics have changed. Processes can be put in place to ensure alignment is maintained and employees will focus on what's most important. For example, a manufacturer switching its focus from preventative maintenance to predictive maintenance must focus on adjusting training, availability of technology, and the way people are recognized. Will there be any changes to the compensation model? What will be the new metrics across teams? The entire system has to be analyzed, changes must be effectively communicated, and scorecards and REPs must be updated.

- What categories need to be added to your balanced scorecard?
- How can you more effectively measure and communicate the metrics that matter and the company's progress toward achieving those key metrics?

FOCUS ENERGY ON ALIGNMENT

There is an assumption that all leaders are aligned and fully engaged when a company rolls out a new strategy. This isn't always true. Earlier, we discussed the importance of sitting down with senior leadership and making sure they all have the same definition of what success looks like—that there is true alignment. Issues arise when individual leaders prioritize their personal initiatives and agendas before those of the organization. Too often, when we first meet a leadership team to help them accelerate performance, we hear leaders say things like "I understand we need to move in this direction, and I'm totally behind it, but I need funding to complete this other project for my division." That. Is. Not. Alignment.

When leaders say they agree with the strategy but still spend time, energy, effort, and probably money (overtly or in hidden costs), working on other things that don't directly connect to the main strategies, they work against a system and culture of high engagement and performance.

To give a specific example, providing undeniable client impact is an important business outcome at SHIFT, and we have clear leading and lagging indicators of success in this area. Each day, we could dream up new product or service offerings, engage in creative business-development activities, or take interest in a new marketing campaign in the company. We field calls from people in our networks who regularly reach out and say, "Hey, let's grab lunch. I haven't talked to you in a while." Unfortunately, every time we devote energy to things that aren't aligned to the most important priorities, we take away energy and focus from the things that drive our primary business outcomes.

- Think about a time when all leaders in your organization were fully aligned on a key strategy or initiative. How successful was the initiative or strategy? (Think about communication, change management, morale, and business impact.)

- Think about a time when all leaders in your organization were not fully aligned on a key strategy or initiative. How successful was the initiative or strategy? (Think about communication, change management, morale, and business impact.)

SUCCESSFULLY LAUNCH STRATEGIC INITIATIVES

Executives can invest extensively in the design, development, and communication of strategy. There is an assumption that if it's designed and communicated well, the strategy will, by default, be implemented successfully. Design and communication do not always equate to flawless execution.

Once a new strategic intent is declared (usually at a big kickoff event), leaders may feel the implementation is consummated. Employees depart with enthusiasm and some level of commitment. However, without specific processes, practices, and protocols in place, people also leave without understanding exactly what changes, what stays the same, and what they need to do to bring the desired change to life day to day, and inevitably, previous ways of thinking and operating stay the norm. The declaration of strategic intent may include a rollout of a new set of metrics, but if context-sensitive application and accountability are not in place and reinforced on a recurring basis, momentum fades quickly.

Most strategic initiatives do not replace the day-to-day operations of an organization. They enhance and add to them, while the recurring regular activity of individual contributors remains the same. When leaders decide and declare a new strategic direction, the expectation is for work systems and all departments and teams to adapt or self-correct based on the proclamation. Changing some key metrics will influence that, but the level of direction must support widespread, sustainable change. Some will leave the all-hands meeting thinking, "I understand the intent of this strategy and the key performance indicators, but tomorrow my team still has to produce twenty thousand units of our product. If the strategy doesn't get implemented, I might hear about it, but if we don't produce the twenty thousand units tomorrow, I will definitely hear about it."

In an ideal world, new initiatives would be implemented smoothly and without business interruption, but many times that's not the case. As an example, when a company has an important HR initiative and the organization acquires another company, suddenly that acquisition becomes the most important thing. What happens to the HR initiative that's been placed on the back burner? How does the organization get back on track with it now that something else has taken priority?

In a thriving organization, successful leaders consider many factors before introducing a new initiative. They consider questions such as:

- How do we clearly communicate the intent of this initiative, in relation to our overall business strategies and goals?
- How do we message this appropriately and offer support?
- How do we make sure we're not confusing people by saying there are multiple priorities?
- How do we ensure that our people, at all levels of the organization, understand what role they play?
- How do we adjust work systems and processes to support the work our people need to do?

Having the answers to these kinds of questions allows leaders to say, "This acquisition is a huge opportunity. We've been working on this for three years, and it's finally come to fruition. This move ties directly to our long-term growth strategy, so we're running with it." That's the time to discuss whether the organization should stop or slow down on other initiatives, and if and when the acquisition requires resources previously allocated to those things. Launching a tiger team to analyze and evaluate options and make a recommendation to executive leadership can accelerate the change-management process. That would also be the time to be overt with employees about how everything is interconnected. For example, with an acquisition, all business-unit goals need to align with, or fit into, this new, larger one. Every department in the organization—finance, operations, sales, marketing, customer service, warehouse, fulfillment, or janitorial—will have balanced scorecard goals linking back to this acquisition. All employees need to understand how they play a part and why the success of the acquisition matters to them, individually.

IN SUMMARY

Organizational momentum comes to a halt when employees can't see how their role fits in with the strategy—distance and disconnection create disengagement and, ultimately, diminished performance. Use the frameworks and approaches we've provided in this chapter to operate with clarity and transparency, measuring what matters most and putting your people in a position to move your organization forward. In the next chapter, we'll address how you can most effectively implement your key strategies.

- Think about a recent strategy or initiative deployed in your organization. How was it rolled out? What worked about the rollout? Where did you see alignment and momentum wane? What did leaders do to get the strategy or initiative back on track?

- List three things you will do to ensure higher levels of success in communicating or executing your next strategy or initiative.

IMPLEMENT STRATEGY

Truth—or, more precisely, an accurate understanding of reality—is the essential foundation for any good outcome.

—RAY DALIO

⚡ CHAPTER 6 ACCELERATORS

RITUALS, ROUTINES, AND RHYTHMS

ENVIRONMENT, SYSTEMS, AND RESOURCES

EXPECTATIONS AND FEEDBACK

CAPACITY AND JOB FIT/MOTIVATION AND PREFERENCES

RECOGNITION, REWARDS, AND CONSEQUENCES

SKILLS AND KNOWLEDGE

Senior leaders of a financial services company often found themselves misaligned on strategic priorities, missing important information regarding organization decisions and not in sync when communicating key messages to their respective teams. This caused frustration, friction amongst the team, and wasted time and resources as they continually put more ad hoc meetings on the schedule to address issues that could have been avoided.

As part of our work with this team, we implemented a new system of planning, including resetting the vision and process for how this team connected. Often, leaders express that they connect well with their leadership peers, dropping by each other's offices, having lunch or a cocktail after work, or having hallway conversations. These things are not the same as setting purposeful time for leaders to get aligned, address critical opportunities and challenges, set plans in place, and hold each other accountable.

The system that we built with our client included:

- Defining reasons why the team should meet
- Grouping those "reasons" into sensible chunks (not all things need to be addressed in every meeting)
- Aligning on the frequency of meetings needed to discuss relevant topics
- Determining which topics could be addressed without a meeting
- Determining who was essential for each meeting
- Determining how to effectively communicate meeting decisions to those not in the sessions

After installing this new system, the leadership team reported increases in clarity and alignment around strategic priorities, less time spent in meetings, and more productive meetings overall.

In the previous section, we discussed how to successfully launch a strategic initiative. In this chapter, we go to the next step, focusing on the critical aspects needed to produce the business outcomes intended from the effort. For a new initiative or strategy to produce the desired business outcomes, leaders and teams need to appropriately adjust the organization's work systems. A new initiative or strategy should become a natural and ongoing part of everyone's work, on every level. Too often, leaders, managers, and frontline employees greet new initiatives with a scarcity mindset to their work. People in this headspace think about the time, energy, money, or staffing they lack. In a thriving organization, people think, "This is a new opportunity for us to make a good business even better. I know my work is influenced by the overarching direction and strategy of the organization, so I need to appropriately shift my energy, time, and focus to support this new direction. Let me think about the best ways to do that." Can you imagine the impact that just that shift of thinking would bring to your organization?

When a new initiative or strategy is first announced, we see email communication deployed, posters and banners hung in offices, and project teams working to build excitement about the new "thing" that is happening. As part of a normal process, teams or department leaders must implement the new "thing" within their groups. Part of the problem is that those asked to implement the strategy don't have the span of control to ensure that each facet of the work system—the six influences—can be adjusted.

New strategies need the highest level of sponsorship. Top-level leaders need to account for changes to the compensation model, adoption of new work processes, elimination of barriers, and reallocation of resources to appropriately support the new strategic direction. Senior leaders are responsible for the coordination of microscopic changes to ensure the new strategy leads to a thriving workforce and an organization that meets or exceeds its goals and expectations.

Think about the last major initiative rolled out in your organization. How was each of the six EPS influences adjusted or
considered to support the initiative?

- Expectations and Feedback

- Rewards, Recognition, and Consequences

- Motivation and Preferences

- Skills and Knowledge

- Capacity and Job Fit

- Environments, Systems, and Resources

ACCELERATE IMPLEMENTATION IMPACT

A high-tech client we work with has been implementing Role Excellence Profiles (REPs) for about twenty years with an increasing
level of commitment to the model we describe. They have added a
role-specific, matrixed approach to create and support an aligned organization. They have role excellence leaders who support integration
and alignment for specific roles. These are full-time roles that own
the responsibility for facilitating alignment across all of the EPS influences and across the enterprise.

The role excellence leader facilitates a community of practice for everyone in that role, gathering input from employees about what is going well and what could be improved. People in a role have an advocate
and channel to share best practices and elevate issues or problems.
The leader has different weekly, biweekly, and monthly conversations
with role members and interfaces with the staff functions supporting
the role. They integrate and coordinate the role across the entirety of
the organization. The goal is ensuring that the role is fully integrated
and aligned with the strategic direction of the enterprise.

Role excellence leaders don't control the six performance influences—they serve as a liaison between the people in control and the people who have needs within their role community. For example, if a company made a decision to roll out a lean manufacturing model, new monitoring systems will be introduced on the manufacturing floor to support the lean implementation, and training may be required; a change in scheduling may occur, and HR must negotiate this in an updated contract. The role excellence leader for the skilled-trade workforce, representing electricians, riggers, and those who maintain equipment, must track these needs and act as the interface with key influence owners.

The role excellence leader will make sure the performance management system continues to align with compensation. If certain tasks or behaviors are no longer needed or new skills are required, the leader identifies them and ensures that training is adjusted and provided appropriately as the processes and procedures are implemented. They will modify and pull together the work system, raising the probability of full implementation in a timely fashion.

SEEK OUTSIDE GUIDANCE

Many organizations believe if they have the smartest people on their teams, they can tackle everything on their own. Organizations that begin with an entrepreneurial spirit and experience tremendous growth often take pride in the knowledge and skill that exists within their organization, and they should. However, business, technology, customer preferences, and how we consume information are all advancing so quickly, it's impossible for people within complex business environments to have all the knowledge and skill required to sustain a thriving organization without additional help. It's a business imperative and a healthy practice to seek insight from sources outside of the organization, because people within an organization are too close to systems and processes to clearly see what may not be working optimally. Perspectives are limited, no matter the diversity in thought or backgrounds.

Organizations also don't have the capacity to provide the right level of support for massive transformation and change. Whether it's the implementation of new technology, a sales force transformation, or a cultural integration, leaders have a full-time responsibility to deliver results for their organization—they can't be responsible for leading another initiative. Having leaders drive a critical initiative with a fractional focus is a recipe for failure. If your company is operating under the premise of creating a thriving organization where the people and the business can reach their full potential, leaders can't do their day job and simultaneously lead critical initiatives. Help is needed.

Many organizations come to us because they need our expertise, but they also need capacity, bandwidth, more hands, and more brains. It is neither reasonable nor prudent to exponentially add complex work to an individual's work and expect that she will be at her best. An individual may be able to take ownership of a major strategic initiative as a collateral duty, get through the work, and see the project through to fruition, but we can assure you that the person and the business will absolutely not deliver the maximum business value.

There are also situations when people are promoted and expected to maintain their previous role. We saw this happen recently at a private bank. The team leads were responsible for supporting and developing financial advisers while still maintaining a portfolio of client assets. A large percentage of the desk heads' compensation came from the strength of their personal portfolio; almost none of it came from providing leadership to the advisers. Since assets drove compensation, desk heads spent most of their time taking care of private clients rather than working with advisers.

This structure was punishing high performers—they were given more and more, and it's a surprise none of the team leads cracked under the pressure. We worked with this bank and it led to a restructuring: the team leader role became predominately a management position with compensation tied to team performance, not just their personal portfolios. This had a radical impact on their organization. Leaders were now able to increase their focus on growing the next generation of successful people.

GET IN SYNC

Implementing strategic change requires systems-based thinking; deliberate planning; laser-focus; purposeful, coordinated execution; rich feedback; and continuous improvement. When an organization operates in complete synchronicity, it can be compared to the most masterful ballet production, symphony, or theater production. It's as if time becomes suspended, work becomes effortless, and each person involved surrenders to something far greater than herself. Close your eyes for a moment. Think about the most beautiful performance you have ever experienced. Feel the energy. Remember the chills you felt during the experience. Revisit the sense of excitement and sheer joy that pulsed through your veins. That is what it feels like when you successfully land strategic change, when you and your organization truly thrive.

It starts with establishing a BEAT.

RITUALS, ROUTINES, AND RHYTHMS

In studying high performers in various roles across a multitude of industries, we know that each has a specific way of thinking—a certain mental model for how he approaches not just work, but life in general. This also exists at the team, business unit, and organizational level. Part of this mental model includes establishing rituals, routines, and rhythms.

RITUAL

Organizational ceremonies, used as methods to deepen connection and embed company values. This could be a specific way to celebrate success, debrief a won or lost new business pursuit, or how new team members become immersed into an organization's culture.

ROUTINE

This could be a specific sequence in which a person prioritizes important tasks, or a structured team meeting used to advance a strategic initiative.

RHYTHM

This could be the operating cadence (frequency and duration) of one-on-ones, team meetings, or performance-based discussions.

 Download at thrive.shiftthework.com/accelerators

CASE IN ACTION

Some enterprises establish rituals, routines, and rhythms in such a deep and meaningful way that they become operating norms for everyone in the organization. A good example is what one of our clients calls their rhythm of the business. There are certain meetings that occur each quarter and recalibrations that happen annually. Performance management is spread throughout the year, and employees know what will happen each month and each week. The entire business operates with structure and routine; the checks and double checks occur on a regular basis, and proper accountabilities are in place. Establishing a rhythm of the business will create a broad, absolute rhythm within the company as a whole, while also developing sub-rhythms within the business units and teams. The result is an aligned company culture that has accountability embedded within that model.

We helped this client create "leader playbooks"—interactive tools that contain current schedules and events on the horizon. When is the budget adjusted? When are staffing strategies and allocations to be completed? What three priorities are leaders accountable for in the month of February? These playbooks allow leaders to see what is expected of them and what will occur during any period throughout the year.

VARIETY IN ROUTINES

When engaging in exercise, there are three variables that help our minds and bodies make consistent progress: frequency, intensity, and duration. Changing any one of those factors will alter an exerciser's experience and results. The same concept applies to our work systems. Altering the frequency of our one-on-ones or team meetings can change the results yielded from those meetings. The simple frequency shift sends signals about the critical connection between the meeting content and the organization's strategic priorities.

A client of ours considered themselves to be a high-performance organization. By many lagging indicators, including revenue and profitability, that claim had merit. However, after starting our relationship with them and digging deeper into the organizational fabric, we saw a variety of foundational areas of concern. These posed threats to their long-term growth. Many of the issues could be traced back to a lack of alignment at the senior leadership level.

To a point raised earlier, it wasn't that their senior leaders outwardly disagreed on what was important to foster growth: engaged employees, improvement of new sales, and retention of existing clients were a few of the common areas of focus. Members of this team got along well, socialized outside of work, and had a deep passion for their business, their people, and their clients. They often talked one-on-one, handled escalated issues as those issues arose, and were fairly adept at fighting fires. The issue was that there was no strategic rhythm or purpose in their connections—they often didn't take time to slow down to ensure all of their efforts were well coordinated and that employees across the organization heard the same message about overarching core strategies and how their personal roles connected to those strategies. This resulted in mixed messages, confusion among frontline employees, and, as a result, confusion for clients and prospective clients.

In short order, we facilitated a process that enabled them to create a new operating system that included a set of rituals, routines, and rhythms and fostered deeper connection, tighter alignment, and performance acceleration across the organization. To illuminate how straightforward this approach can be, here are a few examples of what was installed by this organization:

Weekly Routine: Every Friday, senior leaders conduct a thirty-minute around-the-table call, regardless of where leaders are physically located or how "busy" they may be. They discuss each person's top priorities leading into the next week, their key accomplishments that align with strategic goals, and what help they might need. It's important to note that these calls are not problem-solving sessions. If a team member needs help, he calls it out, and follow-up occurs outside the framework of this routine. The important point isn't that they have a weekly meeting, but rather the commitment to clarity, focus, and alignment forged as an outcome of the connection.

Monthly Routine: Senior leaders convene for a deeper, more strategic session. They discuss what is on the horizon and where they are in terms of strategic priorities. Agreements in these sessions include what does and doesn't need to be communicated to the field, when, and by whom.

Quarterly Routine: This is a half- or full-day off-site, digging into long-term strategies. Bigger-picture ideation takes front stage, considering company goals and changes in the competitive landscape. A segment of the session also focuses on increasing leadership skills.

Because each meeting serves a distinct purpose, the sessions have a different frequency, intensity, and duration to drive key goals and strate-

---

gies forward and to keep the lines of communication open so everyone is informed and stays well aligned. You can use the above framework to refine, revise, or replace your current meeting structures.

USING RITUALS, ROUTINES, AND RHYTHMS TO CONNECT AND ENGAGE

We all have rituals and routines in our lives—some are essential for us to live the best lives we possibly can. For example, quality sleep, a balanced approach to nutrition, and regular exercise provide a solid foundation for healthy living. Endless studies underscore the power of dedicated time for reflection, mindfulness, and gratitude. Within an organization, putting these practices into play helps people more effectively connect to their most important priorities, their passion for their craft, and the purpose they find in their contributions. As leaders, it is our role to create an environment with systems in place, where people can be as good as, if not better than, they intended to be on the day they began their role.

Some leaders think this is soft, fluffy stuff, when really, it is what will fuel most people and get them charged up in their work, also keeping them clear and focused on what matters most. To build and sustain a thriving organization, leaders need to build these routines and rituals into how they run the business.

For example, when starting a team meeting, you can revisit organizational values and the vision, and recognize a team member who recently brought them to life in an interesting or meaningful way. Depending on the rhythm of that meeting, everyone can take a minute to share gratitude for a teammate. Think about the extra energy that people will have when they leave that kind of meeting, as opposed to how they feel after one of your meetings today. The sentiment about existing meetings is likely something like "There's an hour I'll never get back..."

There can also be rituals that are specific to off-site meetings. Maybe everyone gets a journal or a book, and at the end of the gathering, each person writes a note of appreciation or gratitude to the others in the group. A small and important ritual like this can foster engagement, connection, and appreciation. Random acts of kindness and words of encouragement cause levels of serotonin (the feel-good chemical in the brain) to increase for the recipient, but research indicates the levels also go up for the giver. Levels also increase for anyone who hears or witnesses the words or act. A culture of gratitude and kindness creates a positive work environment, keeps people engaged or "switched on," and helps move organizational strategy forward.

Sometimes leaders get so caught up in logic, numbers, and tactical agendas ("I need to get through all of this information on the meeting agenda!"). Think also about how you want people to *feel*, during

- What are the rituals, rhythms, and routines by which you run your business?
- How do those rituals, rhythms, and routines impact engagement and performance?
- How can you improve your rituals, rhythms, and routines to have even more impact?

and after an interaction, what you need them to *know*, and what you need them to *do*. Centering on those three things and building rituals, routines, and rhythms that support the production of those outcomes will help you transform engagement and performance.

SLOWING DOWN TO SPEED UP

At SHIFT, we often talk about the concept of slowing down to speed up. From a high-performance standpoint, one way we apply this is through minimizing the potential for misalignment between manager and direct report. Effective one-on-one meetings encourage this process. We recommend a weekly rhythm for one-on-ones. These meetings ensure employees are focused on what matters most, that barriers to success are surfaced, and paths to remedy issues are confirmed. With this approach, individuals know leaders support their goals of making progress—of becoming better versions of themselves. This level of alignment and connection increases engagement and accelerates performance.

A specific and effective way to amplify the effectiveness of the one-on-one routine is through the use of more real-time prioritization, engagement, and performance processes. One that we love (and also use at SHIFT) is called 15Five. The name indicates that an employee shouldn't take more than fifteen minutes to complete the weekly reflection, and it should not take the manager more than five minutes to review and comment on the report—that's the extent of the investment.

In only fifteen minutes, employees document their most important priorities and outcomes for the week, all of which should link back to the REP. Can you see possibilities with this powerful alignment? Either 15Five or another process like it will provide an agile way to understand how employees are feeling, how they prioritize, and what they accomplish week to week. When a manager has one-on-ones, there is already an ongoing performance dialogue. Because no warm-up is needed, the live interaction can focus on only the most important items.

Another useful dimension of 15Five is the personal reflection process. The first question is asked on a scale of one to five, with five being amazing and one being not so amazing: "How are you feeling?" Employees can comment and give color to their answer. "I'm a five out of five this week. I've exercised every day, and I've completed all priority items. I feel switched on." As a manager, you'd want to know that. If, over the course of a couple weeks, you see that an employee consistently scores herself a two out of five, you'll want to have a conversation about it. Leaders need to recognize when one of their team members isn't feeling engaged, energized, or as productive as they could be. If you're a midline leader, your boss has access to the reports, and if they see no intervention between you and that employee, your boss needs to have a conversation with you. "How are you engaging your people? We've got someone who isn't feeling great. How are we tapping in and understanding what's going on with them? How are we supporting our team member?"

Leaders can ask other questions to get important perspective through the 15Five platform. For example, at SHIFT, we ask our team members things like "What's your biggest fear at work?" or "What's one tough truth you think the organization hasn't faced?" We want them to give some thought to what they've learned, how they're performing, and ways to elevate performance over the last week, month, and year. We want people to slow down, think, and consider what's happening and what's working. What are they focusing on, and how are they doing? We want them to get their heads right and communicate what leaders should know to foster higher levels of engagement and performance; this supports the maintenance of strategic alignment.

With platforms like 15Five, employees can make issues visible to leaders, and vice versa. Through quick exchanges of information, insight, and inspiration, leaders can foster alignment, provide timely support, and increase the likelihood an organization will succeed.

CASE IN ACTION

One of our favorite case studies involves a consumer goods company. It provides a great example of a successful, integrated startup. We were asked to support them in a "greenfield project"—a new manufacturing facility starting from the ground up. They had no physical space, existing infrastructure, or culture. It was truly a "clean slate." We worked with another consultant on this project whose background was in organizational design and sociotechnical systems.

Integrating the cultural and social aspects of a technical environment provided challenges. When the architects and engineers were designing the plant, part of their consideration from day one was creating an optimal workflow so the workers could identify with two strategic customer groups. The design took into consideration what was important to retail customers when they purchased the product and what really mattered to retailers who distributed and sold it. Since the design was sensitive to these two audiences, the individuals in roles within the plant would know if their primary accountabilities were to the customer or to the retailer.

Why did it matter that the two audiences were served differently? Consumers wanted all bottles to be filled to the exact same level, caps to be put on at the same degree of tightness, and labels to be applied neatly. The distributors wanted boxes that didn't collapse when stacked to a certain level, and the contents of the box to be made crystal clear, even when the boxes were on pallets above floor level.

The differing standards for these two audiences were built right into the process design, role definition, training, and KPIs for the plant. The workforce was split into two groups: one filling and labeling bottles, and the other packing and shipping. The compensation models were built to reward the maintenance of quality standards for the two different audiences, and the messaging about the value of their work was communicated and embedded into the way they were hired and trained. All of this carried over into expectations and the feedback they received from management.

The equipment at this plant was also designed in a new way. This company had other plants where the equipment was used in isolation, but at this facility, it was set up in a fully integrated process. We talked with high performers from the older plants and then worked with the engineering staff to develop training for the new single-flow process. The job design, hiring profiles, training, process design, leadership and management, and the compensation systems were all fully integrated into this plant from construction, to startup, to full implementation. It was truly ideal.

With the brand-new plant, we were engaged very early on, and that was critical for its success. The performance system wasn't an add-on or an afterthought—it was part of the overall structure and operation of the plant. The company didn't finish building and then figure out how to fit people in. Rather, it developed a thorough and complex design of the work system as an integral part of the plant. This dream scenario doesn't happen often.

Another unique—and nuanced—characteristic of this project was its organizational politics. Leaders didn't see this plant as simply a new location. They wanted it to be an exemplar for future plant designs. There was an enterprise-level commitment to fully integrate the people component of the overall process and work system. With a capital project like this one, there usually aren't any extra dollars to go around; the physical act of building a plant, the acquisition of technology, and inevitable delays consume all the money. In this case, the commitment to do everything right was reflected in the budget—funds were allocated appropriately for the design and implementation of a "barrier-free" work system as part of the overall project budget.

It's often presumed that if the process and technology are right, people will immediately conform to whatever is put in place. If the right people are hired, good technology, good process, and good talent will then achieve "flow," or a state of total alignment. The difference between what occurred with this project and most other projects we have supported is that it was approached as an integrated system with the level of support necessary to put all the pieces together.

This ideal implementation isn't limited to startups or the building of new facilities. You don't have to start from ground zero to create a thriving organization—there are opportunities for process improvement and increasing employee engagement within existing companies. SHIFT has a documented, repeatable, and scalable process that works, no matter the stage of the organization.

MAKE IT REAL

The above scenario was an ideal implementation, but how can leaders handle the ones that are less than ideal? When creating a new strategy in an existing company, leaders face the challenge of adjusting previously established compensation models, workflows, accountabilities, and cultures. Many factors and questions that would not apply to a startup or brand-new company need to be considered to position the strategy or strategic initiative for the best chance of success.

The president or CEO owns the responsibility of establishing the vision for a new company strategy or initiative, for setting new expectations, and for creating alignment of the six influences. She is also responsible for ensuring the appropriate adjustments are made and for mobilizing other leaders to make changes necessary to effectively land the strategy. At the new strategy's inception, she begins by putting together a project team consisting of key players so they can all get in agreement with the new strategy. After the team is assembled, the team leader needs to spearhead critical thinking to determine how to adjust each of the six Exemplary Performance System influences for maximum performance impact. Here are some questions you can use to prompt the right kind of thinking.

ENVIRONMENT, SYSTEMS, AND RESOURCES

- Is new technology required for successful implementation?
- Will this impact staffing levels?
- Do we need to reallocate existing resources?
- Will we need outside support?

 Download at thrive.shiftthework.com/accelerators

EXPECTATIONS AND FEEDBACK

- How will this change metrics for new and current employees?
- Do we need to update the job description?
- Do we change the performance management system?
- Will leaders need to shift the way they coach employees?

Download at thrive.shiftthework.com/accelerators

CAPACITY AND JOB FIT/MOTIVATION AND PREFERENCES

- Do we need to create or update Role Excellence Profiles?
- Do we need to refine job interview questions?
- Are we prepared to possibly shift current employees into new roles that are a better fit?

⚡ Download at thrive.shiftthework.com/accelerators

REWARDS, RECOGNITION, AND CONSEQUENCES

- What impact will this have on the compensation model?
- What are the other ways we can recognize and reward performance?
- What will the consequences be for underperforming?

⚡ Download at thrive.shiftthework.com/accelerators

SKILLS AND KNOWLEDGE

- Will this change the tools we use or the processes for producing expected results?
- Will new-hire training need to be updated?
- What training will be required for current employees?
- How will we measure proficiency in any work or outcomes that shift?
- How can workers support their own performance?

⚡ Download at thrive.shiftthework.com/accelerators

IN SUMMARY

While we have shared sample questions that can be asked during strategic changes or new initiatives, leaders need high levels of discipline and a rigorous approach to follow-through and execution. New initiatives will not deliver the intended benefits with a fractional focus or effort. Leaders must set the example of full commitment to an execution and implementation effort that delivers the intended business outcomes.

We have used the EPS model across many industries, from high-tech to financial services, manufacturing to retail, and across numerous roles within each of those industries. When a role or a team is accountable for results, the model applies. Without accountability for results, roles, teams, and organizations underperform. In either case, the EPS model can bring to light the most direct ways to shift performance.

RESISTANCE AND RESILIENCE

The best way out is through.

—ROBERT FROST

 CHAPTER 7 ACCELERATORS

PRECISION COACHING

"I think it is going to take at least five years for us to see this transformation through and start to realize the full impact," our client said. I remember this conversation as if it were yesterday.

"BOOM. He gets it," I said to myself. As we said at the start of this book, business transformation is some of the hardest work that leaders get to do. It takes guts, perseverance, unwavering commitment, exemplary leadership, and robust change management. Our client could see many of the potential land mines, organizational turf wars, fixed mindsets, and competing priorities that we would need to work through in order to make the progress needed to successfully drive the company's strategic goals.

This is the kind of vision and leadership required to successfully land complex initiatives. Don't you know that five years into our work with the client, they were setting company revenue records, expanding into new product and service offerings, had completed new business acquisitions, and saw consistent improvement in many areas of their employee-engagement survey scores. And they were hungrier to improve even more and to take on more transformational initiatives. BOOM. BOOM.

We look at various factors when studying change readiness in organizations, including self-perception of skills, capabilities, performance, and bringing company values to life. We also give people the opportunity to rate colleagues and managers on the same factors. Interestingly, most people view themselves more positively than they do others. Even though the surveys we do are completely anonymous, we could attribute some of the variance to hubris—that people rate their own skills and performance highly. This tendency seems especially reasonable if employees think that the surveys aren't really anonymous and that their bosses will know who said what. Who in their right mind would say that they lack the needed skills to perform well or that their performance was suboptimal? This example is a symptom of a main issue that undermines transformation efforts, engagement, and performance: one's MINDSET.

There's a concept in social psychology called fundamental attribution error (FAE). It says that we attribute the reasons people do things based on how we imagine someone else is reacting to a circumstance. If somebody doesn't return your phone call, FAE could lead you to believe that they are blowing you off or being rude, not that they are on vacation or—possibly—sick. The person who cut you off in traffic is an ignorant jerk, operating recklessly. Your conclusion doesn't consider the possibility they were rushing to the hospital for an emergency. We often attribute behavior without understanding the real cause or reason behind that behavior. We condemn others yet offer grace to ourselves—we imagine the worst intentions of others, and the best for our ourselves.

When organizations don't leverage a framework like the EPS when implementing significant change, fear, uncertainty, and doubt arise. People resist sharing their knowledge, fearful that they could become expendable. They believe that what they know begets job security. People resist admitting to knowledge gaps for the same reason. Lacking the right environment, rewards, recognition, and consequences, individuals at all levels become more risk-averse, thwarting innovation. They believe that failure will lead to negative consequences. With companies that lack change readiness, we often see a "blame and credit" culture, where individuals fight over credit when things go well, and are quick to point a finger at others when things go awry. Tough to build a high-performance culture with this mindset. In fact, only about 15 percent of people can make the changes, find work-arounds, and bubble up as high performers in these environments. This small subset of a team responds well and finds ways to be successful when facing unmanaged change. However, most people will feel overwhelmed, underequipped, and resistant, and will default to what they have always done, day in and day out.

Some leaders believe change is like a magic pill that will create an instant miracle. This new system will radically change our customer relationships and accelerate sales! It doesn't. Change is more like starting a program to improve your fitness and health as a beginner. Along with adhering to an exercise program tailored to meet a person's specific goals, the individual must sleep and eat well, stretch, and manage stress as part of the systematic approach to becoming more fit and healthy. When they do, it may take six to eight weeks for visible results to begin to appear. Even though people know this intellectually, they exercise once and wonder why they haven't lost weight or why they aren't already stronger. There is a big gap between expectations and reality.

What really happens after the first day of exercising? Within twenty-four to forty-eight hours, soreness, stiffness, and discomfort set in. Individuals resist going back for another dose of exercise; discomfort becomes pain, and results still haven't shown up. The same mindset applies when it comes to resistance to organizational change—people have tried change, and it hurt. It was awkward, confusing, and may have revealed limitations for what people know and can accomplish. Who would want to experience that again?

These beliefs, feelings, thoughts, and emotions can accelerate or decelerate change and initial success. Introducing collaborative change instead of imposed change can make the difference in mindsets and attitudes—it all comes back to engagement. In this case, that means setting proper expectations about the challenges the effort to change brings, so people can appropriately prepare for what lies ahead.

Many baby boomers wanted to retire around 2007, but the financial crisis left them unable to afford it. Those individuals stayed in the workforce due to necessity, not because they wanted to keep working. This group, and others in similar circumstances, clung to the value they had developed through years of experience. If they gave up knowledge or insight by training new, younger employees, they would be giving up their source of power. They might lose their relevance, get fired, or be forced to retire before they were financially ready. Unease caused by uncertainty in the workplace isn't limited to tenured folks. Think about employees entering the workforce or joining a new organization. It takes courage and resilience to share knowledge, admit ignorance, learn a new culture, and create value. While the individual certainly bears responsibility for managing these parts of himself, leaders bear responsibility for creating barrier-free environments in which onboarding new employees occurs as seamlessly as possible.

Leaders must have the social awareness and emotional intelligence necessary to understand the root causes of resistance. Baby boomers are far from the only workers who fear losing their value. By understanding this fear, the process of change can be designed to relate to human spirit, energy, and connection. Organizations can do a better job of energizing employees and creating environments where they can be their authentic selves, able to express vulnerabilities and fears—knowing that their leaders will support them through the process of change. In the case of 2007 and the baby boomers, leaders could have (and some probably did) meet with employees that were close to retirement to align with them on their current condition and situation. Together, they would be able to find ways for those employees to offer high levels of value to the organization, including transferring knowledge to new hires and serving as mentors or training buddies for a period of time that served all parties well.

PRIORITIZE MINDSET

Part of the impetus in starting SHIFT was our fascination with human performance. Specifically, we wanted to understand and help employers harness the power of why some people could achieve and sustain high levels of performance, while others' performance rose and fell. We began by focusing on sales organizations, because their performance often had the most visible and significant impact on overall business performance. In our studies, we found that, while business results and processes were very important elements in establishing solid performance, those two factors alone did not produce high levels of output on a consistent basis. Something was missing. Over time, we came to realize that MINDSET was the missing piece of the puzzle, and developed the SHIFT Achievement Model (see figure 7.1).

FIGURE 7.1

THE ACHIEVEMENT MODEL

Download at thrive.shiftthework.com/accelerators

We will apply the model to an example we all can identify with: New Year's resolutions. Every year, one of the most common resolutions is to lose weight. For this example, we'll use a resolution to lose ten pounds. Applying the Achievement Model, the specific resolution of losing ten pounds is the desired **result** (the top of the pyramid).

Individuals who aspire to lose ten pounds can leverage various **processes** to attain that outcome. These include, but are not limited to, exercise, intermittent fasting, joining Weight Watchers or Jenny Craig, or surgery. Regardless of the chosen processes, people don't usually stick with weight-loss resolutions. They gain and lose weight repeatedly. Weight is like finance in an unhealthy way: when you gain it back, it comes with interest, and there's a reason why all of this happens. Focusing only on results is not a long-term solution—the results may be attained, but they aren't sustainable. Even many of the winners on shows like *The Biggest Loser* regain the weight they've lost. The difficulty sustaining change has been proven time and again, whether the goal is weight loss, quitting smoking, or implementing new ways of driving sales and operational processes. The missing element, again, is **MINDSET**.

There is a growing body of work on the subject of mindset, with one of the early thought leaders being Carol Dweck, who authored a book on the topic. Mindset is shaped by our beliefs, and our beliefs are formed from two things: past experience and future choice. Past experiences can be good or bad—you believe something to be true because you've had an experience with it before. Maybe you've tried and failed at exercise many times, so the next time you join a club, you'll join the cheapest one out there. Why? Since you believe you will fail again, at least you will save money. This is a limiting belief or, as Dweck calls it, a "fixed mindset." A more empowering belief (what Dweck labels a "growth mindset") is "I'm going to succeed this time because I'm going to choose differently." One example of an empowering belief in action comes from one client's salesperson we met who had never done sales in his current industry. He had no experience that indicated he would or could thrive in his role. Even so, during his interview, he told the hiring manager that he was going to be their number one salesperson. He got the job and aligned his beliefs and behaviors to that of a high-performing salesperson: he studied other high-performing salespeople, adopted some of their good habits, asked customers what they valued in the relationships with those sales professionals, and read many of the same trade publications the top performers were reading. He had far more than a positive attitude; he took ownership of developing the skills and knowledge needed to build his capacity and draw job fit influences from the EPS to increase his likelihood of success.

Here's another example. Think of when you made the decision to have your first child (or maybe to adopt your first pet). You had to create a mindset around a future choice. You had no experience to prove or—perhaps—even suggest that you would be a good parent; you chose to be a parent, and you shaped a belief about yourself that you could be a good one. Your belief, in turn, led you to do certain things to become what you saw yourself as capable of. The mindset you chose enables you to do things that are aligned with the outcome you envisioned, creating a winning equation.

MITIGATE RESISTANCE

Change can be met with resistance when people have a fixed mindset and they anchor their beliefs to bad experiences in their past. These experiences could include their boss having said that certain things would come to fruition that didn't. Some people have seen so many unsuccessful attempts that they now view any change as the next "flavor of the month." When employees don't trust that change will be real or safe (or real safe!), they tend to operate with the aim of compliance instead of being inspired to commitment. They do just enough to not rock the boat, but not nearly enough to help the company achieve strategic change.

Much like the barnacles that grow on the hull of a ship create drag and slow it down, resistance to change lowers the efficiency of an operation. Resistance rises in the absence of effective communication by leadership, and/or the organization doesn't measure success in terms of the full implementation of a new strategy, product, or technology.

Success is *full* implementation of the new strategy, direction, facility, or system and the fulfillment of its benefits to the enterprise and support of employees. We do not believe there is innate resistance to change, making the presence of resistance optional. When the benefits to the customers, employees, and organization have been communicated effectively, resistance is neutralized, if not vanquished altogether.

Resistance can be subtle and passive, or it can be obvious and active. When people believe that change is being imposed upon them, the discretionary effort they give at work begins to wane. While most people will not consciously or purposefully undermine the change, they will not have the same level of motivation or commitment to its success. When highly engaged individuals first accepted their position, it was most likely because they bought into the purpose of the organization and their role, and the associated value it produced. Significant change that comes without appropriately engaging team members through the process can leave people feeling like they suddenly have a different job—one they didn't sign up for. They may stay with the organization out of necessity, because they need the income or health benefits, but their level of excitement decreases.

Those who resist passively spend time doing nonproductive things rather than focusing on high-value tasks to drive the business strategy forward. Active resistance comes when change conflicts with something an employee values or when the employee does not understand why the change is important.

Changes—unintentional and intentional—that trigger or amplify resistance include:

- Increases in the number of hours people must work or the amount of work they must take home with them. People focus on what they did historically and ignore what they're being asked to do under the new change. They might think, "I never worked this many hours before, and now I'm working harder than ever."

- When employees are asked to do something they don't feel good about. A publicly traded bank recently incentivized people to add unnecessary solutions to product portfolios to hit company sales goals. This resulted in employee lawsuits—people claimed they were fired because they refused to add the unnecessary and unrequested solutions—an active form of resistance. (Note: We agree with the resistance in this case, because what the employees were asked to do was wrong.)

All people within an organization need to be front and center in the change process. People inherently like to have things done with them versus to them. Practically, they need to know how to function in the new world being created. All six influences in the EPS, including Environments, Systems, and Resources, must be aligned with the new definition of success. Preparing people to thrive as a result of the new strategy, technology, or product release can't be thrown in last-minute before (or after) a multimillion-dollar system goes live.

Employees need to know how the change helps them do their work more effectively, helps their customers do or get what they want, and better enables the company to fulfill its mission. People need to know how their daily tasks align with organizational priorities and support the desired outcomes. When employees do not understand the purpose behind change and its value to their work, disengagement, distraction, and distrust all increase. These are massive forces against which leaders need to work every day. Yeah, shit gets real. The good news is that there is a better way.

Think about a recent change initiative that failed to deliver the intended business impact and results.

- Where did resistance show up?
- When did the resistance surface?
- How was the resistance handled?
- What will you do differently next time?

BUILD RESILIENCE

Thriving in a role at work and—more broadly—in life requires deep resilience. Resilience is the ability to bounce up off the proverbial mat and rebound—quickly, effectively, and with a productive mindset. At SHIFT, our study of resilience reveals that it stems from a person's clarity about and focus on what is truly most important to her. This is what provides the extra fire to make that one more phone call to a new prospect, to have that difficult conversation with a direct report, or to engage that customer who you know is massively dissatisfied with your product or service. The "match" that lights each person's fire can vary. It's important only that we find one and we use it. In our health and fitness story, the "match" may be the deep desire to be alive to see your grandchild graduate from college that gets you out of bed and to the gym every day.

The declaration of one most-important, nonnegotiable business goal starts the process, but it can't end there. As described above, a person needs to get clear on why the goal matters so much. We use an exercise with clients called 25 Reasons Why to establish the reasons why they are working toward a self-described nonnegotiable outcome.

When facilitating this exercise at a national sales meeting for a global client, we asked the group of 150 people to write down their nonnegotiable, most important business goal for the coming year, and to list the twenty-five reasons why that goal was a nonnegotiable. Participants were then asked if they would like to share their answers. One shared that her "nonnegotiable goal this year is to hit X amount of revenue in my territory." We asked for her top three reasons why. She gave us reason three, and then reason two, before sharing reason one: "My granddaughter's parents died, and I am now her caregiver and guardian. I need to put her in a place of financial stability and security; I don't ever want her to worry about where her next meal will come from or whether she'll have a roof over her head." WOW. Think she woke up every day with a clear sense of purpose and drive? You bet she did.

Coming to work with that clarity of purpose is much different than coming to work and thinking, "I'm here to make fifteen phone calls and schedule three sales appointments." This reason gives this individual extra drive and commitment in her work. When resistance shows up, her underlying driver helps her find the resilience to push and fight through challenges. It helps her to successfully overcome not feeling like making another call, overcoming an objection, preparing for a meeting at the eleventh hour, or adopting a new system of change imposed by the company.

Figure 7.2 highlights common aspects of resistance and resilience. As a leader, it is critical to understand that these aspects exist for all of us. You must be able to engage in productive conversations with your people to help them understand, embrace, and work with and through these issues and opportunities. You can have these conversations as part of your one-on-one cadence with direct reports.

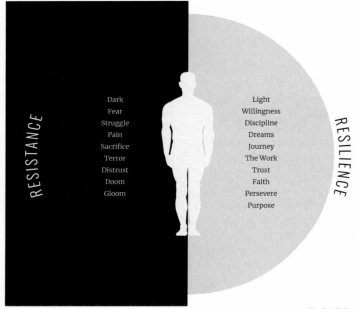

RESISTANCE

Dark	Light
Fear	Willingness
Struggle	Discipline
Pain	Dreams
Sacrifice	Journey
Terror	The Work
Distrust	Trust
Doom	Faith
Gloom	Persevere
	Purpose

RESILIENCE

FIGURE 7.2

LEVERAGE THE REP TO ACCELERATE CHANGE

Having the right governance and implementation team and an integrated systematic model can avoid some of the resistance we described in the previous sections. We encourage leaders to have REPs in place for all critical roles—the ones that are necessary for success of new strategies or initiatives. If there aren't any high performers in a new process or strategy yet, extrapolate excellence from the process or strategy itself. Determine at which level the roles will be impacted, and adjust the REP accordingly. Will a current accomplishment be eliminated or replaced? Will new accomplishments be introduced? Are the excellence indicators for each of the accomplishments being impacted? Will the job become easier or more complex with this change?

The REPs can be redesigned based on the change in strategy or direction. Once that's been done, look at the six influences and answer the questions from the end of chapter 6—the REPs reflect the anticipated impact of the change at the individual role level. After updating the REP, make any needed adjustments to the work processes associated with each of the influences to remove unintended barriers to higher levels of performance.

Measure, assess, an adjust as you go. For example, if robust user-acceptance testing isn't possible prior to the introduction of new technology, it's imperative to collect feedback after day one and over the near term following the change. You'll want feedback from people who are closest to the work. This will help you avoid some of the most common pitfalls of new technology system rollouts, when employees say things like "Who designed this system? It doesn't make any sense. Leaders have no idea how we do our jobs." If the system indeed is flawed, employees will develop workarounds to survive. They in no way will be thriving. This extra work needed merely to tread water is due to what the company does to their people with poorly designed and executed systems and their rollouts. We'll say that again: not what the company did for them, but what the company did to them. There must be a feedback process, and it can't be limited to day one. Be ready to receive and incorporate feedback on day two, day twenty, and day two hundred—all enabling leaders to make agile adjustments when and where it makes sense.

Read your Instagram and Facebook feeds, listen to your friends, and soak up the chatter at networking events or the next cocktail party you attend; when people comment on their job, you'll see and hear comments that include:

- "Same stuff, different day."
- "Just trying to make it through the week."
- "People around me don't care, so why should I work harder?"
- "I can't believe the boneheaded decisions our leaders make. I'd do it so much differently if I were in charge."

People are running to the weekend and then dreading Mondays. Countless frontline employees and middle managers, directors, and even vice presidents we've met feel powerless to effect positive change in their organization. They've lost hope and are resigned to believing that the way things are is the way they'll stay. They don't trust that management will ever make it better. You now know, however, that it can be different and how to make it so.

LEVERAGE FACILITATORS

PRECISION COACHING

The best performers commonly have a coach, someone whose primary purpose is to elevate performance. In the workplace, it might be a direct supervisor. High-performing individuals may ask their manager to support their attending a sales meeting and to debrief with them afterward. They may be asked to review a new operational improvement proposal to poke holes in the logic or to do a skill-building dry run in which they listen to their direct report prior to making a presentation to a client. This intentionality and repetition of effort, along with the insights and reinforcement from a coach, leads to higher levels of individual and organizational performance.

We previously outlined how organizations can use the REP as the design point for formal and informal learning interventions. One of those interventions is coaching. What makes SHIFT's coaching approach (Precision Coaching) so effective is the use of an outcomes-based approach to determine the relevant areas of learning and action. Too often, we see leaders and managers apply general coaching tactics to elevate performance. They might choose to work to help their direct reports improve critical-thinking skills. This could be a useful area, but the general approach lacks context sensitivity and thus appropriate emphasis. Instead, leaders need to consider the primary accomplishments outlined in the REP. With those primary accomplishments in mind, the leader can coach her direct report to apply critical thinking in a way that increases the likelihood that the primary accomplishments will be produced more consistently and with higher levels of proficiency.

 Download at thrive.shiftthework.com/accelerators

Developing your learning and development specialists into REP process advocates will inspire and enable them to partner with your leaders to tailor specific approaches to facilitating precise development.

SHIFT PRECISION COACHING MODEL

ENSURE CLARITY ON DRIVERS OF HIGH PERFORMANCE

On the outset, coach and client ensure there is clarity and mutual understanding of what drives high performance within the client's role/desired role

- Include input from client's manager or other senior leader
- Supported by the Role Excellence Profile (if available) or other source

MEASURE PROGRESS AGAINST GOALS

Continually assess for coaching success throughout the coaching relationship or engagement

- At the conclusion of each session
- At the midpoint of the engagement
- At the conclusion of the engagement

ALIGNMENT	ANALYSIS	ACTION
Coach and client align on coaching goals and outcomes for each session	Explore presenting challenges and determine root cause (skill gap/application)	Coach and client co-create solutions aligned to goal achievement
Focus conversation on solving problems related to long-term desired outcomes	Create space for awareness, insights, reflections, and observations	Client commits to action and tests new strategies and approaches
Direct the conversation towards the most high-value topic(s) for the client	Evaluate progress to goal (outcomes, mindset, path, strategies)	Client solicits feedback from stakeholders on ongoing performance

Thriving requires clear-eyed perspective. An external view like the one SHIFT provides to our clients is essential to help you from beginning to believe your own BS. Think of Enron. Did people know Enron's senior leaders engaged in bad activity? Some probably did, but others may have thought their leaders would never do anything wrong or intentionally harmful (this goes back to the cognitive biases previously outlined). The same could be said about Bernie Madoff or Jeffrey Epstein. Generally viewed as nice men, nobody would think they would cheat people out of billions of dollars—or worse.

Those are among the more extreme examples, but left unchecked or unchallenged, a little wobble here and a blind eye there, and pretty soon, you're in a whole heap of trouble. The dynamic perspective gained through teaming with an outside resource ensures that your organization will receive ongoing, focused, and objective feedback. You'll benefit from honesty and truth-telling specific to the areas that are most important to your organization. In addition to telling you what you need to hear about these critical areas, your progress and success are measured against a crystal-clear target—such as shifting performance, Net Promoter Score, reduced downtime, or gross sales.

Only working with people internally risks a highly homogenous way of thinking. Leaders fail to foster productive debate, decision cycles spin endlessly, and they don't hold peers accountable. Whatever it is, outside accountability pushes people to productive levels of discomfort, fostering growth and improvement. The right partners won't let you get away with statements like "But we're so busy here." When the right external parties are involved—those with the expertise you need and by whom you feel properly challenged—you're much more likely to experience success.

IN SUMMARY

Get your head right. That's the big point of chapter 7. As we've shared multiple times throughout *THRIVE*, it is hard to successfully land business transformation and change efforts. In order to bridge the gap between strategy and execution, leaders need to understand that providing steadfast leadership amidst chaos, clarity and certainty during times of great ambiguity, and fortitude when it would be easier to relent and retreat are defining characteristics that form the foundation of a high-performance culture.

To help you in your endeavors, we strongly recommend that you have people in your life who can, among other things, tell you what you need to hear, not what you want to hear, and get you to see points of view and possibilities that you may not have otherwise been able to see. These people can be mentors, peers, or friends, but you've got to have folks who can play these roles for you if you are really going to be the leader of a thriving organization.

In our concluding section of *THRIVE*, we will help you distill all that you've learned into a clear action plan, propelling you toward leading the high-performing company you envision. It is time to bring that vision to life.

CONCLUSION

No amount of security is worth the
suffering of a mediocre life chained to a
routine that has killed your dreams.

—MAYA MENDOZA

 CONCLUSION ACCELERATORS

WRAP

You've read *THRIVE*. Now what?

Based on extensive experience, we know that the EPS can accelerate change and translate strategic initiatives into business impact and results that align with intended outcomes.

Through this book, we have exposed to you to new ways to build a high-performance culture and have given you access to frameworks, tools, templates, and examples that you can put into action now. Applying the mindset and processes outlined in this book will help you produce cross-functional integration, clearly defined initiatives and strategies, and the barrier-free work systems and processes to bring the six performance influences into alignment.

If you want things to be different—if you are *really* ready to commit to elevating performance and business results in a sustainable way—you must take ownership of the change you need to see. You get what you tolerate. The success—or lack thereof—in your business and your life is mostly within your control. This book may have disturbed you, having brought you to a realization that what you've been satisfied with is no longer okay. You see that it's time to commit to a different approach. Leading your people past their current plateaus will not be easy. In fact, it will be painful, risky, and met with resistance. That doesn't matter, because you know you can be more, do more, and give more. Every successful person has a mental model for accomplishment. The intent of this book is to help you develop your own. *THRIVE* is our effort to provide you with a replicable, scalable model to achieve levels of success that you didn't believe possible—for your organization, your people, and your customers.

Just as you completed the MAP to set intentions at the start of *THRIVE*, we will take you through a closing reflection ritual, called the WRAP. Please answer the following questions:

- What are your breakthroughs, insights, and greatest learnings?
- What specific actions will you take to put those breakthroughs, insights, and learnings into motion?
- How will you directly contribute to producing a barrier-free work environment?

⚡ Download at thrive.shiftthework.com/accelerators

The world needs you to take the next step. Put your new ideas and knowledge into purposeful, consistent action.

"Good" results put you out of business. "Great" results keep you in the middle of the pack. Organizations that *THRIVE* set new standards for business.

The universe is going to give you

the exact same

lesson in different

versions over again

until you master it.

This is one of the single

most important laws

you can learn about the

nature of reality.

Everything else builds upon this.

—MARYAM HASNAA

ACKNOWLEDGMENTS

You fight for me. You are my champion, my agent, my cheerleader, my muse, and my true partner in life. You hold me accountable to the standards I set for myself and others. Your belief in and love for me fuels me to change the world every day. JoAnn, we are on an incredible journey together, and *THRIVE* is one part of bringing our vision to life. Thank you for your unconditional love and being my unending source of inspiration.

For my mother, Vicki, who always encouraged me to speak from the heart, showed me the value of hard work, modeled what it meant to always do the right thing, and encouraged me to make my dreams a reality. I remember learning from you as I helped you grade math and English papers, celebrating with you as you taught me to ride a bike, struggling with you as I found my path when graduating college, and dreaming with you as I envisioned the ways I could contribute most significantly to the world. Goldstein women have always been the rock in our family, and you've been mine, every step of the way.

Joe Mechlinski, you told me how hard and rewarding writing a book would be. When we got the band back together at SHIFT, this was part of our master plan, and you have been an essential part of this journey. You knew I had a story to tell and insights that could help to change the world, and you were unrelenting in your support and encouragement. My brother, we are kindred spirits in so many ways, and I am thankful that we get to change the world together. I've got your back, and I know you've got mine. We are truly just getting started.

Paul, we've been at this one for a while, and I couldn't be prouder of what we produced in *THRIVE*. Thank you for being a great colleague, an inspiration, a friend, and a remarkable human. Ready to get to work on the next one?

Jeff Lesher, this book wouldn't be the same without your contributions. I appreciate your counsel to own our expertise and to be direct in how we guide leaders to build thriving organizations. Staying humble and sharing expertise don't have to be mutually exclusive.

No strategic initiative achieves full potential without killer project management, sharp branding, and impeccable execution. Tara Fox, you nailed all of these, and then some. Thank you for your advice, insight, and expertise helped to bring *THRIVE* to life.

Scott Francolini, Joe Schriefer, Steve Pruett, and Mal Poulin, thank for being a part of *THRIVE* before Paul and I even started formally writing. You've experienced the approach and impact, and we appreciate your thoughtful contributions and endorsements of the work.

To every current and previous member of SHIFT Nation, each of you has played an integral role in *THRIVE*. You bring the methodologies, frameworks, and high-performance philosophy to life every day, helping leaders transform their organizations. You inspire me to reach higher, dream bigger, and move our mission forward with passion and purpose.

People come in and out of our lives, and I know that each interaction happens for important reasons. Jennie Phillips, you inspired me to write, challenged the way I think, and pushed me far outside of my comfort zone, and for these things, and many more, I'm eternally grateful.

Jose Presbitero, I could have used another fifty years with you here in this world. Your humor, humility, kindness, and love inspired me to create better versions of myself, give endlessly and without judgment, and always serve. I know you are still with me and JoAnn, and I appreciate the invisible and tangible guidance you give every day.

For every leader who aspires to build a high-performance culture, you inspired me to write *THRIVE*. I see your heart, hustle, and humanity, and applaud your courage to do the hard work needed to shift the way work is done.

Benjamin Zander. You were the keynote speaker at a global leadership conference I attended, and your messages still ring true. We get the opportunity to make it all up every day—all of it—and so why not create what inspires us, what drives us, what lights us up?! This is my mindset and approach every day, and I cannot thank you enough.

Made in United States
North Haven, CT
24 March 2022

17500180R00126